FINDING S̶

Truly inspiring in every way! Dorothy Gray has written a piece of literary work that explodes with the anointing of the Holy Spirit. This book should be on every believer's daily devotion list to read! Awesome work, inspiring and uplifting in every way!

~ Bryant Corbitt, Program Director, KMX/106.7

Dorothy Gray has been able to show the beauty in one's journey from pain to power. She has been able to use a voice of calamity and hope to show God's plan for each one of us.

~ Dr. Uzoma Uwakah

Reading this book has truly blessed and encouraged me. It speaks volumes to the heart.

~ Tripta Cohen, Registered Nurse

Dorothy Gray takes us on an incredible journey from brokenness to victorious breakthrough. Sharing her story and faith lets us know, even in brokenness, what ever is left God can use to raise up a champion. If you should read at least a hundred books in your lifetime, this should be one of them.

- Apostle L. Martin Mull, Pastor, Teacher, Speaker

Praise for
FINDING STRENGTH IN BROKEN PLACES

As I read Dorothy Gray's book I could feel the very fire that was shut up in her bones. I could step precept upon precept upon her words, which are grounded in The Word. Her faith shined through as only one that had walked through the wilderness and now has reached the Promised Land. She makes others know that there is empowerment and peace in our despair as the Spirit speaks to your heart.

~ Jonathon Thunderword, Pastor
By the Way Ministries

Knowing Dorothy Gray professionally and personally for years is inspiring in itself. It has been a personal blessing to know her.

~ Kelli Harden, Chief Executive Officer

Dorothy Gray has walked through the valley of the shadow. In fact, she spent quite a lot of time there in her earlier years. But her strong faith gave her abiding courage, and now she shares that message of courage, along with her story, in a book that's sure to uplift you.

~ Cynthia MacGregor, Author

FINDING STRENGTH IN BROKEN PLACES

Your Destiny is Far Greater Than Your Experience

DOROTHY GRAY

This is a work of fiction. Names, characters, places, and incidents are the products of the author's imagination or are used fictiously. Any resemblance to actual events, locales or persons, living or dead, is entirely coincidental.

FINDING STRENGTH IN BROKEN PLACES

Words and Images Copyright ©2016 Dorothy Gray

Photography by Arjay Moreno

All Rights Reserved.

ISBN-13: 978-1535074322

ISBN-10: 1535074329

Library of Congress Control Number: 2016910912

FINDING STRENGTH IN BROKEN PLACES

DEDICATION

This book is dedicated to my mother Naomi Graham, who is with the Lord. Because of the things that you endured throughout your life, you were a woman of courage, forgiveness, humbleness, and quiet strength. When your time was up here on earth, God took you home to rest. Needless to say I miss you more than words can say. Yet my soul rejoices knowing that you are in the presence of the Lord, free from all the pain and the cares of the world. You can walk along the streets of gold. You were "a legacy of Love."

In memory of my godmother Dorothy Williams. Prayer Warrior. You were there praying for me, loving me, nurturing me, and most of all caring enough to carry the weight of my pain in your bosom. It was your fear and admonition for the Lord that you would rejoice and shout. You rejoiced in the Lord here on earth, now you are rejoicing in eternity. You were "My Angel."

To my aunt Annie Woods, how can I ever say thank you? You are always there for support, strength, guidance and most of all your infinite wisdom. I call you Blessed. You are "a Woman of Wisdom."

Finally, thank you Holy Spirit for the anointing and guidance in writing this book. Thank you Father for being the sustainer of my life, allowing me to walk through the different seasons of my life in Victory.

10/29/16

DEIL:

Prosperity and
Abundance
is All around
you. The gift of time

Allows you

Endless

possibilities

FINDING
STRENGTH
IN
BROKEN
PLACES

Wowthy
Gray

Your
Destiny
is
Far
Greater
Than
Your
Experience

FOREWARD

In the realm of pain and adversity, many face battles that threaten to overwhelm us and those that we love. Finding Strength in Broken Places is about a woman's unfailing journey to wholeness and healing. The book brings clarity and understanding to the broken pieces and broken places of our lives. As you began to peel back the layers of your past, you will understand your present. You will understand how to break the cycle of generational strongholds, addictions, weaknesses where invisible chains seem to bind and hold us in bondage.

In this book, you will find your answer. You will marvel at the awesomeness of God's grace, his irresistible, indescribable love for us and his faithfulness. God will go where you can't go, do what you can't do and reach where you are unable reach. Know that you are not destined for defeat, no matter how dark the valley gets or frightening that it may seem. Know that you are destined for greatness. This book will inspire, empower and encourage you to never quit.

I Speak To Your Heart

A Letter from the Holy Spirit

While you are Standing at the crossroads of your life, wanting, longing, asking, hurting, confused, unsure of the next step to take, past mistakes, present pain, asking for understanding, clarity, protection, wisdom, guidance, breakthrough, salvation, shelter, love, wanting more, needing more, asking for more, not sure which way to go on your road to a place called Destiny. If you can open your hands to receive, and lift your arms toward me and say, "Yes," there is a letter waiting for you:

Oh how I have longed for you to reach for me. I want to be that light in your life that leads the way for you. I want to be the safe harbor that holds the anchor and the lifeline in the time of trouble. I am your way back home to me. I want to speak to your heart. I want to download not the presence of the world but "MY" presence into your heart. Oh how I have yearn for you, to sup with you, and have great companionship with you. I cry for you -- you have turned from the things of me to satisfy your flesh, and the cares and desires of this world. My love is so great, and my arms are stretched wide to receive you unto myself. I have sent you a comforter which is the holy spirit to guide you, teach you, and bring you into all truth. Give me your hurt, give me all your pain, past mistakes, your brokeness that you are still holding on to, struggles that won't go away, your physical and emotional issues, loneliness, oppression, depression, broken dreams, buried memories, despair, sorrow, hopelessness, disappointments, tragedy, grief. As your pour your heart out to me, I the lord thy god will fill you with my peace. The peace that I give doesn't bear explanation. Allow me to be the peace that speaks to your heart and bring comfort to your soul in your darkest hour, and when you find yourselves in those dark places. Allow me to be the peace that covers you when fear shows up. I see the cries of your heart. In the midst of it all, when you feel that you are alone, know that you are never alone. I am always with you never losing sight of you, holding you up, loving you beyond what you could ever think or imagine. Even when you can't trace me, feel me, or hear that small still voice, I am there. I am with you making a way when there seems there is no way. My hand is there to guide you, strengthen you and protect you.

I allowed you to be placed in painful places or that dying place in your situation, circumstances, that would serve as your testing ground to build your spirit, strengthen you, restore you, and place you in right position with me- (Close to the father). I am divinely orchestrating to draw you close to me. I am a God of Perfection. "Come, let us return to the lord; for he has torn us, that he may heal us; he has struck us down, and he will bind us" (Hosea 6:1) I will make it good.

Give me your heart, and watch me wash away the debris that have been clouding your heart and mind. You are not alone. I have a plan for your life. My Child, I am the one who died on the cross for you. I am the one who gave my life for you. My hand is upon you. I am here for you. I give sight to the blind. I will bless you, give you strength, and a renewed mind. Trust me. I will never leave you. I am all you need.

~ The Holy Spirit

"For I know the Plans I have for you," declares the Lord, "Plans to Prosper you and not to harm you, plans to give you hope and a future." Then you will call on me and come and pray to me, and I will listen to you."

~ Jeremiah 29:11-12

Pain

"The Lord is close to the broken hearted; He rescues those spirits are crushed."
~ Psalm 34:18

Throughout my journey in these past few years, God has allowed me to travel to different cities, states and countries, and to connect with people from different cultures, races, beliefs (religious, educational, political) with different issues and with different ways of responding to problems based on their experiences.

There is one thing that we all share in common, regardless of our color, nationality, religion or the background we come from. There is one thing that we all experience, or have experienced in life, pain. Emotional pain. This pain can be inescapable and also indescribable. It's severity and it causes, however, as well as the way we react to it and cope with it, differ in each of us.

Pain can be short-term or it can remain long-term. But in any case Pain is... well, Painful. It is tough to cope with. Some pain can cause us to feel that we are on emotional life support with no way out, but to stay connected to, or whatever or whomever is causing the pain in the first place. We allow ourselves to stay on Emotional Life support as a result of remaining in places of darkness far too long. Pain can imprison our minds to the point that we end up in such places. We have allowed ourselves to be turned into the person God never intended us to be. We allow our lives to be controlled by others pushing the button and dictating the way aspects of our lives should be.

We remain on life support from the pain of carrying weight from past issues daily issues, cover-ups from the past, unaddressed issues and emotional toxins. You may ask what are emotional toxins? Anger, bitterness, self pride, negative thoughts, jealousy, buried memories, regrets, resentment, hatred, shame, self-loathing, guilt, unresolved conflict and the list goes on. Soon the weight of the pain can become so severe that it causes the well of living waters that springs from our souls to become dry, leaving us dehydrated and desolate. We become like a ship without a sail seeking a river of living water that can bring life, relief from our pain and, most of all, freedom from our situation.

Pain will cause us to question ourselves: Where do I go from here? How do I fix this? How did I get in his place? How do I find that place of peace? How do I get back to the place that I once was so happy?

"I am hurting!" This thought, this feeling places us on an emotional track from which we travel on a diversity of paths, trying to unravel and make sense of it all. Yet in most cases we don't understand why, nor are we equipped to embrace the pain when it first presents itself. As a result, it can send us on paths that we didn't know were lying dormant within, but rose in the time of pain. These are paths of destruction and the deeper the pain, the greater the path of destruction can become. It leaves us trying to unravel and make sense of it all and not understanding why.

Pain comes with no warning labels. The hardest pain is the pain you never saw coming without warning. We never had a chance to brace ourselves for the hit. You are left devastated, confused, shaken, not sure what hit you. It slows you up, then shuts you down. It leaves you in a place asking, "What just happened?" and "Is this real?" When the pain shuts you down, you now have come to a place where the emotional pain becomes buried. Buried pain does not die, it festers. So in order to maintain an emotional equilibrium, we bury it. We convince ourselves that it never happened. We try and find balance and keep up with the demands that we face on a daily basis.

Pain can become so intense that it resembles a growing, consuming inferno, slowly burning out of control. The deeper the pain, the more it burns and the more out of control it gets. Some of the deep wounds may be: rape, incest, childhood violations, abuse, tragedy. Soon it sends us on a path of destruction leading to the doorstep of weaknesses and addictions.

The weaknesses turn into an aggressive form of cancer that takes over your life and then trickles down in the generation line, causing generational curses, family pain and struggles. The addictions leave you in situations of bitterness: anger, abusive, infidelity, sexual promiscuity, drug addictions and eating disorders; all as a result of your efforts to suppress the negative thoughts and emotions that are causing you the pain. When you wrap yourself in the arms of addictions and weaknesses, they will show you just how powerful they can be.

Pain can cause us to become numb on the inside. You feel empty. The sign that points to the heart reads Null and Void. The tragedy or the real danger comes when you have become lifeless or motionless in your pain. When everything has grown cold and numb, you stop caring, you stop feeling, communication starts to cease and you become disconnected from the pain. It becomes a sign of death. Pain is the sign that there was still life and you are able to express how you feel. Yet for all the damage pain does to us, we have a tendency to ignore these signs, thinking that this will all go away. It won't. What this continuous pain does is weaken your spirit man. It becomes a living organism, slowly eating away at you and moving toward destruction. It will wreck your dreams and keep from achieving your goals. Worst of all, it will sabotage your relationships, causing distrust. The pain that we carry causes us to mistrust others, including those we are in close relationships with. We have allowed pain to drive us to actions and decisions that goes against the Will of God. This pain has imprisoned us, robbed us of our hope, talents and accomplishments.

Pain can cause you to attach yourself to things and to people that are unhealthy for you, and the things around you. And this all takes place in the interest of wanting to feel accepted and needing the pain to go away. You do something that is self-destructive or self-degrading, which may feel good for the moment or right for one night. It may make you feel important and bring back memories, or you may think it will make you forget about your pain and your past. But it doesn't. At best, it's nothing more than a temporary patch. At worst, it adds to the pain and exacerbates it and you are left with feelings of suppression, insecurity and depression.

We suppress those feelings, trying to forget what is really plaguing our thoughts and emotions. We have lost ourselves, lost sight of who we are as a person. You find yourself having an identity crisis. So you try and skip over the pain, work around it, get past it and somehow just get through it, without really addressing it, embracing it and dealing with it.

We live out our lives on a stage, actors in a play, pretending all is well, pretending the situation is other than what it is. When we are around family and friends, we take the show. We are show-stoppers and happy problem solvers. We play the part of team players that can handle anything. While we are on the stage, we believe the role ourselves. But, when the curtain comes down and the stage lights are off, all those hidden issues, which had been lying dormant, surface. Eventually the pain becomes too strong to stuff way any longer and instead takes center stage becoming our main attraction. What was once our private pain now becomes our public platform.

Some of us deal with pain through inward storms or should I say silent frustration. Inward storms cause emotional and mental surges, which beset our mind and spirits. We have a tendency to blame outside stuff on inside turmoil. We become enslaved to anger and bitterness. It sneaks into our soul quietly and unobtrusively becomes mistaken for deep thinking or just concentrating. Many times it is like hypertension, also known as the silent killer. It doesn't show itself until it has done collateral damage. You don't feel the effects until it is too late. The pain remains buried and the individual appears outwardly in control, never revealing the storm that is plaguing him or her inside until it is too late. The end result can be lethal! If this describes you, you live your life in sadness as a result. Your life should be a time of happiness and rejoicing. You want to feel whole and at peace, but yet remain torn. "Someone is home, but never happy."

Pain can cause us an array of emotions that we don't understand. So we are left pulling from resources of other people's emotions, experiences and how they have dealt with pain in the past. We also find ourselves dealing with pain as a result of a generational line. This is the way Big Momma or our aunts, have dealt with pain and this is the advice that she brought to the table. Yet following her example doesn't help. It leaves us still broken, confused, guilty with the question marks plaguing your thoughts. "How do I feel safe?" "How can I make it through this situation?" "Will I get through this at all?" "How do I get back up after the fall?"

We have gone as far as doing self-harming actions to numb our pain when we felt it was too much to bear. So we turn to addictions. We turn to sexual promiscuity, shopaholics, workaholics, we get mixed up in gambling or we fall into drug or alcohol addictions, all in pursuit of numbing the pain, all in an effort to feel good about themselves. But these are mere band-aids applied to the gaping wounds of pain that plague our emotions. And all these misguided efforts still leave holes in our hearts. By temporarily numbing the pain through self-destructive behaviors, we become enslaved to these behaviors in our pursuit of relief.

Substance abuse: we saturate the body and dull the pain. They become our drug of choice. We like how we feel for the moment. Eventually, what becomes our social, feel good narcotic turns into a chemical dependency. We depend on it chemically to take us to a feel good place or a place of "I want peace." The more the pain and the void chases us, the more often and the faster we chase the high, no matter the cost of the relationships with family, friends, jobs, careers, our dignity, integrity, character and most of all ourselves. Soon, you become detached from what truly is facing you, while the addictions have become attached to you. These addictions have destroyed homes and torn families apart.

Addictions soon teaches you their ways, "I want it, no matter who and what I hurt, by any means necessary. I will turn you against the very people that love you. I will enslave you and cause you to turn away from God. I don't live for truth in you, but a lie. Why? Because I need to cover up what is truly plaguing my soul. I'm in a dark place. I will cause you to be wrapped in the arms of the weakness that you have opened the door to and the temporary pleasure that it brings. It shows itself as a comforter or a buffer between you and the pain. It keeps you from dealing with the pain. Each time the pain shows up, you band-aid it with your choice of "PLEASURE." I take over your mind when you leave me in control. Soon I own your soul till I destroy you.

Sex: sexual temptations, sexual perversion, pornography, multiple sex partners, affairs. If that is your form of narcotic, gets you between the sheets and takes you emotionally to a place of temporary pleasure, so you want it over and over again, as it temporarily leaves you forgetting about your pain and what is truly plaguing your soul. You will find yourself with a voice of reasoning, trying to find the right mate that will make "you" happy for the moment. You are held captive and your dreams and goals are even further out of reach than before.

What was once the spark that ignited your soul with motivation and determination slowly starts to burn away. You are unable to move forward and instead find yourself reaching back, trying to figure out "Where did it all go wrong?" and "How did I end up here?" Instead of building up your life, you've attached yourself to things and behaviors that destroy it all in the name of wanting to feel good and numb your pain.

How do you find that place of tranquility and peace? What is my purpose in life? Why are you here? Why did you have to go through this? These are the questions that you find asking yourself. "I didn't deserve this. I need peace." I have lost the fire that once burned inside of me with determination. "How do I get it back?" "What happened to me?" "I need to find my way back." "I feel like there is no way out." "I have lost my passion and zeal for life, how do I get it back?"

When I feel like I am stuck and there is no way out, I accept. I accept the pain, but I am still broken. I accept the abuse, but I remain confused. This pain has become an entrance into my life with no exit sign leading to my freedom and peace of mind. "So I died." My spirit died trying to win in situations that I thought would bring me truth, yet it left me with no hope. I thought this would bring me closer together with someone else, but we remain so far apart with no closure.

I died with my soul playing a symphony of emotions: broken, confused, lonely, defeated, a victim instead of victorious, feelings of "I can't, I won't," "Never have and Never will." I don't have the strength to fight the things that I don't understand. Each time

I get up with just enough strength to fight, life knocks me down.

I died accepting this way of life called "Stuck." I feel stuck in situations beyond my control. I died trying to grab hold and give birth to my dreams.

I died to things in my life in which I vested time, energy and my heart. Yet despites the investments, I feel empty. I have many deposits with no withdrawals. My emotional account is marked "Insufficient". I am left broken, angry and trying to figure it all out. I am left pulling from resources that I have no knowledge of. My emotions are running rampant. Anger and rage are setting sail on my emotions.

I died to situations that I never signed up for: tragedy, loss (bankruptcy, financial losses), illness (diseases that have left me with a poor prognosis and life expectancy marked "Death"), barren. "Why me?" It wasn't supposed to be like this. This is not the way life should have been.

The pain and the trauma of things that happened in our past remain as fresh in our minds as when the incidents occurred. A war soon breaks out inside of us. We wrestle with these infirmities until we become emotionally handicapped. We master how to numb the pain. We soon attach ourselves to unhealthy relationships that become toxic. We sometimes become desperate, rummaging through other people's lives and using them as narcotics. The deeper the pain, the stronger the narcotic has to be. We soon move from one form of emotional narcotic to another trying to numb what is truly going on inside us, until we become damaged goods, living our lives out with major drama at the forefront. We feed on Drama, we nurture Drama and soon we live for Drama. Anything that upsets them triggers drama. Why? Because they have a wounded soul. The anger and the pain from the wounded soul refuses to be pacified. So the storm rages into drama. Drama becomes the forefront of our everyday lives, till we find that we are Damaged Goods.

Many times our soul can become wounded from secret sins to open sins: infidelity, divorce, adultery, rejection, fear, self-hate, holding grudges and "I am never good enough." We reject who we are because we don't like who we are. We don't like who we are because we don't know who we are in Christ. Our self worth becomes thrown in the ashes. Our mindset causes us to feel that we are not good enough, inferior, unworthy and unloved. So we start rejecting our self. Once we start rejecting ourselves, we cause a rip between our Soul and Self.

Sometimes the pain is so intense, and yet the intensity has resulted in heart attacks, emotional or nervous breakdowns or suicide. We then start producing physiological symptoms within our bodies. Many physicians now have a diagnosis for it, called Chronic Pain. There is no real origin of where the root of the pain is coming from when you present to the physician with the same complaint over and over, but yet multiple diagnostics tests are negative. Many times when stress triggers, the body goes through flare-ups or exacerbation of the physiological symptoms to the point that it can cause crippling effects or better yet cause them to become bedbound until the exacerbation decreases or ceases. Pain medication becomes the buffer to help the person deal with the physiological pain. Autoimmune disorders (origin unknown). The body began to attack the healthy body tissues. Depression is sometimes anger against itself. When anger becomes repressed for so long, it shows up in a form of depression. With anger and bitterness, when not properly channeled or expressed, it doesn't go away. It becomes displaced exhibiting itself in self-destructive behavior. Guilt may be an indicator of feeling trapped. The pain has not been addressed. Many have built walls as a form of protection from the pain or the trauma and the memory of it. They have built personal altars in their mind where they can hide behind, which manifest itself in their split personalities. They start to form different personalities.

"A double-minded man is unstable in

all his ways,"

~ James 1:8

Many have committed suicide not to end their life, but to end the pain that they are in.

My thoughts and my emotions have now become a symphony of events that plays over and over in my mind, adding new verses to an ongoing song. Each time a new situation arises and the pain deepens, the song becomes louder and louder, till the volume of it shatters my world.

Not only did my world become shattered, I became shattered, emotionally and spiritually. I don't have the strength to fight the things I don't understand. So I accept whatever life places in front of me.

"Satan uses every means to keep us preoccupied in introspection or stuck in compulsive ruts. We end up enduring the lives of quiet defeat, not free to focus on redeeming the unreached."
~ Tom White, Author

THERE ARE TWO TYPES OF PAIN IN THIS WORLD

PAIN THAT HURTS YOU

or

PAIN THAT CHANGES YOU

III

Finding Your Purpose In Your Pain

The level and the intensity of our pain differ inside each of us, for obvious reasons. We haven't had the same experiences, haven't endured the pain as long, aren't predisposed to not being able to healthily regulate our sadness and rage (two common reactions to pain) amongst other emotions, we don't have a good support system, our tolerance for pain (the threshold at which it becomes too much for us to carry without it crippling our daily lives) these are just a few of the reasons why the nature of our pain, the experiences we have in how we feel it and how we react to it, are all different. We all turn our pain into power differently, some taking longer than others, going further downhill before turning around than others, or accepting reality quicker than others.

Sometimes, instead of doing the work, allowing ourselves to embrace pain (that is to say, accept the reality of the pain, attempt to find the lesson behind it, move forward with the knowledge in healing), we become wrapped up in, entrapped by and made a slave to our pain, it being a terror that haunts us both awake and asleep. Mind and soul are contained in the body, so it is only natural then, that the pain within us causes problems in the physical or tangible realm.

We can begin to experience physical pain as a result of carrying the emotional pain around inside of us silently for so long. We may instead take to trying to alleviate the pain through paths of self-destruction, often in the form of powerful, crippling addictions; drugs, sex and gambling are but a few. Or we may develop night terrors, not even allowed a sweet, peaceful fantasy, before awaking to the nightmare once more. Most of the time we don't even realize why we are struggling with issues. Sometimes it takes years for us to admit we have a further problem! That's because we haven't even admitted why are hurting, or that we even hurt!

We have not given ourselves permission yet to know and accept that whatever we have to endure in this life, we will rise above it. We find ourselves hit with a hurricane of distorted thinking and negative emotions. We have spent most of our time in the painful situation digging through the ashes and the mud of the no's, not embracing the resounding yeses. We have not given ourselves permission to move forward and heal. "How much longer will we carry on in agony? When will we finally say enough?" Many times we may find ourselves asking the question,

"What good will come of this?" We must remember that there is a greater plan that God has for us. Pain has purpose.

Before we can find Purpose in our Pain, we must first understand "What is Pain?" In order to help someone get through the pain, we must help them understand pain. Pain, Latin word: pay, punish, torment. Pain can be experienced on different levels, from mild to unbearable. Pain can be physical (sickness), emotional (rejection, loneliness, broken hearted from loss, divorce, abandonment), psychological (depression, anxiety, anger), financial (lack, indebtedness) and spiritual (nightmares, tormenting spirits). We are fighting to be free, yet not understanding what we are going through. We spend countless hours asking the question, What is going on? Why do I have to go through this? Many times fear creeps in and takes its place leaving us to think that we are left alone in our darkest hour. What we don't understand, we fear. What we begin to see in front of us is: defeat, loneliness and the circumstance that is facing us with no way out, but to give up, give in or die, emotionally, in the pain.

"Pain Has Purpose."
~ Romans 8:18

In writing to the Romans, Paul asserts "our present sufferings are not worth comparing with the Glory that will be revealed in us." Pain was the component to carry out God's divine plan for growth and increase. The real question lies with us. Number One: Will we walk with God? Or walk away from God? Number Two: Will he make you bitter or better?

Pain builds strength. Before a diamond can be called a diamond, it has to be put through a process of immense amounts of pressure and tremendous amounts of heat in order to be perfected; the same applies to Gold. Fire does not destroy gold, it purifies. Nothing brings luster to your character and commitment to your heart like pain and opposition. The finished product is a result of fiery processes and a furnace of afflictions. The same thing happens in our everyday life. We must be put through a process of shaking, shifting and molding. We were designed to survive, finish strong and stand strong. We have to remind ourselves that we will be okay. The coal doesn't doubt that the process it has to endure that will make it a diamond.

Why should we doubt that God would give us anything more than we can handle? No matter what happens, you can handle it. All you need to do is give yourself permission. Know that God loves us, comforts us and helps us in the time of our pain.

"God is your present help in the time of trouble."
~ Psalm 46:1

We must never allow our pain to consume us, forgetting who we are, becoming someone or something else, losing ourselves. It's a distraction to our destiny and the greater things that God has in store for us. While our actions become the seeds of our deeds of the future, our focus must be on the present, on reality -- not on distorted thought processes and loss of self. We cannot allow ourselves to become lost in the pain, to lose to the pain. To do so, is to die, plain and simple. Take even a natural death of old age, what is it but the loss of one's self in pain? All of life is pain, after all, death is only the escape from it.

Never allow your pain to push you into an identity crisis. It's a distraction to your destiny and the greater things that God has for you. Do not confuse these truths. Life is worth living. Your actions become the seeds of your future, but your focus must be the realty of now. When you are pushed into an identity crisis, you are not dealing with the pain properly. (If at all to deal with something is to take care of it, to eliminate it (to use "street language"). To be dealt with is to have the pain control-and yes sooner or later, eliminate you! Ignoring a problem is not eliminating a problem, do not make the mistake either.) but allowing the pain to dictate our destiny, as we go through stages, phases and masks, dealing with the newfound self destructive habits we've formed, instead of taking the path of healing-the path of your power.

Your pain becomes a testimony to you and a platform to another person's destiny. Consider the stories of our personal heroes. Had they taken "the way out of pain," would their names be in a book? Their pictures on a wall? Images conjured up in moments of hurt and fear? So why can't it be the same with us? We may not be in a book or be a name remembered, but we can still affect another's destiny by sharing our pain. This is why we suffer, so others may be helped to survive, or simply continue to thrive, and to be revived during those down and our moments. When someone begins to shine with brilliancy, you are looking at someone who has been through the furnace.

A young man once endured an incredibly abusive relationship, which teetered him on the brink of almost committing suicide on multiple occasions. He was toyed with, manipulated, emasculated, bought to his knees, not knowing what he did to deserve this or when would it end. The man constantly living in the pain of yesterday, unable to move forward in life, wondering why he was made to endure this pain is in his life. He went on to become a teacher and one day he met a young man who was living the very script he had been years earlier and that's when it all made sense. He was able to help this young man and that knowledge gave him Peace. Today he is living happily, doing what he loves (teaching) and has a beautiful wife and child! There is a larger plan than us at work! Indeed the more broken we are, the more blessed we become not in riches, but in Grace, Wisdom, Courage and Strength to overcome circumstances and an unwavering faith that you will always have the victory. Pain is not just a source of empowerment and a catalyst for healing in ourselves and others-even more important, it is a way for us to connect to each other, share our pain, find comfort in, that we are not alone and coming together to share our experience, strength and hope in healing.

Pain alerts us that something is out of place. It allows us to take inventory of our lives and circumstances and people in them. Some people are in our lives for a season and some for a reason. When God wants to take you to greater things, there are other things you must let go of. They can become a distraction and cause you to derail on your road to your destiny. When you become too comfortable, you don't grow. God's intentions are to push you beyond your comfort zone, but not to hurt you. It shakes up your comfort zone enough to move you out of it. Pain is powerful healing and it has to be all the more powerful, to overtake the pain, using its momentum against itself. Pain becomes our power, which in turn empowers others.

Pain unifies Churches, Communities, States and Nations in their darkest hour. It brings them together to stand as one in unity, unwavering with one goal in mind, to ease the pain and embrace others who are feeling the same pain. Beauty and unity comes out of this pain.

"If one part suffers, all the parts suffer with it and if one part is honored, all parts are glad."
~ 1 Corinthians 12:26

Pain purifies our mind and spirit. The beauty in this is God allows us to be placed in the refiners fire to bring focus to what is true and what matters in our lives. When you are operating in counterfeit faith, you will never be able to withstand the pain. Once the impurities are burned away, what is of value will remain.

Pain produces an opportunity for us to experience the Grace of God. Grace gives us the strength to overcome the pain and to be victorious, triumphant in the face of all struggles. Grace keeps us in a state of perfect peace, silent serenity, when there is turmoil surrounding and threatening to swallow us. Grace always works in our favor.

Pain is a pathway to a higher purpose. It points us in a new direction. It opens up an intimate relationship with God. He brings comfort. Who you are, who you are made to be, who you can be tomorrow through healing, is strong enough to bear your pain today.

Before we can understand and change who we are, what we are and where we are, we must first embrace ourselves, for all that we are. The good, the less than perfect and the downright awful. We are greater than our past and strong enough to handle where we are going.

If we choose to push through the pain, fight through the hurt and press through the No's, we can find our true purpose and say Yes to Destiny. We have to trust God to take us on a journey, trust the process and know that God has it all in control.

How can we know God will pull us through? Does he tell us why we suffer?

A perfect answer to this timeless question can be found in Psalms 84: 5-7

"Blessed is the man whose strength is in thee: in whose heart are the ways of them. Who passing through the valley of Baca make it a well? The rain also filleth the pools. They go from strength to strength, everyone of them in Zion appeareth before God."

It's right there in the Word! By trusting God and his word, even while walking through the valley of weeping, at our lowest point, we turn these tears into a well. Sorrow becomes beneficial to our fellow man: Pain is Power! Our pain is to give life to others in their pain! Our hurt gives those around us relief, as our tears also make pools, communal bonding though pain and a way to release this pain! When you can tell the truth about your pain, you give others permission to stand in their pain. It's not what you go through, it is how you come out of what you are going through. The end result if you can trust God in the process; you will not come out empty, but with great substance.

So it is here then, in our pain, in the peace that follows, here that we can finally see clearly. It is here that we start to finally understand and see that our cries were being answered. We were just screaming too loud to hear! This is where we will know the Power of God, the presence of his glory, as well as the Divine Peace we've been searching, endlessly and fruitlessly. We are soon able to rise at last, with a spirit of Praise and Thanksgiving.

"Out of pain and problems

Have come the sweetest songs

And the most gripping stories"

~ Billy Graham

Finding A Voice In Your Pain

Getting to the core of unresolved issues can be painful, but nevertheless all the more helpful. It can start out with a bitter taste, but yet in the end is sweet. Suddenly the rumination becomes useful; it uncovers things that we have been holding onto subconsciously. It helps us answer questions we've been left alone in the dark with for years. Most importantly, it can help us at last come to peace.

Dorothy Gray

Let us examine when our fracture happened. The fracture that attacked our ego and caused us to question our self worth. What was it? What was that particular moment that caused us to feel unsafe and unprotected, scared and most of all, unsure? More often than not, it is from our childhood. These wounds are so well-hidden. Many times the issue dates back to our childhood. As a child growing up, we need to feel protected, nurtured, held and loved. Children need consistency and structure. Without a well-structured environment, cracks are left in the foundation. Cracks that are all too easy to slip through. Once these cracks have formed, the foundation can no longer protect us from harmful elements, leaving us open to debris. Once the debris has made its way into the home (your mind), it goes on a mission called erosion, which is followed by destruction. The debris slowly eats away at the foundation, one room at a time.

When our hearts become broken, that becomes our first initial breakdown. We're then taken on a wild roller coaster ride of emotions. We feel abandoned, unprotected, unsafe and unworthy. This first breakdown starts with a hole in your identity. Who am I? Where did I come from? Did you ever love me? And if so, why did you leave me?

Once a hole is punctured in our identity, the negativity seeps in slowly undetected like a virus. Suddenly, seemingly overnight, we develop negative thoughts and emotions. The deeper the pain, the more negative thoughts start to arrive center stage. You now start preparing to play the leading part in this drama that you have been cast to act in. Other times, we attempt to hide away from it all, but it soon starts to resurface, suddenly, like boiling water in a teakettle. The pain rises to the top when the heat is turned up. We experience further trauma bringing that initial pain, that identity crisis, to the forefront. We cannot receive what we do not feel like we deserve and so we time and time again accept the pain we are given. You can never receive what you feel you are not worthy of. So you accept less.

Why? Because you never learned to uncover, understand and embrace the pain from your past. We feel undeserving of love, respect, honesty, truth and trust. Rather than embracing our pain, we become the manifestation of pain. As we begun to manifest our pain, it starts to weigh us down and consume us entirely. We go to sleep in pain and we arise in pain. Soon it comes to the forefront in our conversations. Our conversations soon become sour. We cry so much that we cannot even muster the energy to vocalize our cries anymore. Sometimes we communicate with others to the point that we feel exhausted after leaving their presence. Pain surfaces. We exhaust ourselves in pain. Yet, still, all the while, we cling to our pain and distorted thinking, convinced that we have it all firmly under control. But it comes to a head, inevitably it always does, no matter how "strong" we think we are. We become fatigued, irritable, paranoid and many times emotionally territorial. The pain takes us over. The more we try to resist, the more the nagging feeling persists, calling us to give in. We try to pretend the pain does not exist, so we live a lie. We find ourselves on the run trying not to deal with it.

STOP!

It's time to stop running from your past. These broken shards of glass that you are still holding on to, causes you to carry a limp into your future. We have to learn to push past our fears and embrace our pain. We must learn to be true to ourselves. Never allow your pain to control you to a point that it incarcerates your mind. More importantly, we need to accept and prepare for the reality that this is a process and not an overnight fix. It is not something that happens overnight.

How do we find our voice in our Pain? Where do we see ourselves in it all?

The latter questions answer the former; it's about our perspective. Before we can even begin to begin the process of turning our pain into power, we must first find our voice. And to do that, we have to examine our perspective and (almost always) change it. Are we victims or will we become victorious? Are we winners or losers? Are we in it still or on top of it? Are we controlled or are we in control? Are we in power or will we remain powerless? Will you walk in fear or will you trust God?

Relationships: wrong people and wrong relationships can cloud your mind and spirit. Do they speak life or gloom and doom? Do they bring life? Show me the people that you hang around and I will show you your future. Lose the ties that bind if it is not empowering you to be better and stronger and to the things of God. Greater is coming.

Power of the Tongue: nothing can destroy your joy and hinder you from change quicker than complaining, negative thoughts, words and conversation.

**"Let no corrupt communication proceed
out of your mouth."
~ Ephesians 4:29**

The power of your tongue holds the key to life and death. Words can minister life or they can bring death. Your words can breathe life into everything around you or it can become the trap that destroys you. Depressing television shows, sensual music and books will surely guarantee your spiritual suicide. You become an actor center stage in your mind and thoughts. Pieces of your past surfaces and you relive them over.

"Mine eye affecteth my heart...."
~ Lamentations 3:51

"Pleasant words are health to the bones."
~ Proverbs 16: 24

Sin: from open sins to secrets sins, sin is what it is and will always be, SIN. It poisons and it promises. Sins promise you roses, but deliver you thorns. Sin promises you life and the keys to what you are searching for in your situation, but in the end, delivers deception and death.

Find your voice of truth and stand strong in it. The key to being an overcomer is to realign your thinking and stand strong in it. We have allowed pain, worry, fear, doubt and distorted thinking to paralyze us from dealing with truth and what is right. Standing in truth becomes the lamp under our feet that lights thy path, where the word of God becomes your comforter, your strength that keeps you standing strong and the compass that guides us in the directions that we must take to that place of peace and tranquility. Truth becomes our safe harbor, our refuge and healing balm.

So the question is, will you stand strong or remain bent in bondage? You cannot stand strong alone. It is the Word of God that will be your strength.

"The Lord is my strength and my shield;
my heart trusts in him and I am helped. My
heart leaps for joy and I will give thanks to
him in song."

~ Psalm 28: 7

"For it is God which worketh in you both to
will and to do of his good pleasure."

~ Philippians 2: 13

"For I know the plans I have for you," declares the Lord, "plans to prosper you and
not to harm you, plans to give you hope and
a future."

~ Jeremiah 29:11

When you trust God's word, you become in agreement with him. It's your affirmation to what God says about you. It's your sure walk to Victory. Victory over insecurity, low self-esteem, self-worth, anger, bitterness, rage, lust, wounded souls, addictions, diseases, pain, lack, or anything that has held you in captivity or bondage, from secrets sins to open sins. When you come to the Father in agreement or should I say in faith, you are willing to give up the prism of lack and limitation and see through a spiritual eye. You are ready to accept the things that are already in divine order. When you are exercising your faith, you are standing firm in truth that you know. You are looking at the circumstances from whatever it may be and declaring that it has no power over you.

When you are bent in bondage, you have not found the freedom to stand straight for which you yearn to be free. Maybe we can identify with the woman in the bible who had to walk bent over with her face toward the floor. For eighteen long years, she had been unable to stand straight or do much for herself. Yet she faithfully attended the synagogue and no doubt became lost in the crowd. Jesus, noticing her plight reached out to her with words of LIFE and LIBERATION.

"Woman you are loosed from your infirmity."
And he laid hands on her and immediately
she was made straight and glorified God."
~ Luke 13: 12-13

In essence, he was saying to her, "No more bondage! You are free! Lift up your head!" No longer does she have to walk with her head held down in despair and her face to the floor. She has found her voice in her pain. Her body was free, her spirit was free and her mind was free. Then she began to Praise and Glorify God.

As we begun to change our perception of pain, refocus our perspective and at last find our voice to say "Enough. No more." When the enemy plants seeds of bad thoughts, resist it. Refuse to identify with the enemy's accusations against you and believe what the Word of God says about you.

Let each new day be new life, for remember, all we have is now. If we cease to carry our pain from yesterday into today, we can enjoy today so much more! We will be able to live a new life FREE.

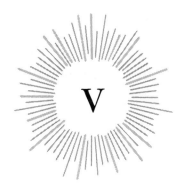

Broken Pieces

"Never Lose Your Identity In Your Circumstances"

As a young lady approaching woman-hood, I was very shy and confused. I had low self-esteem and a lack of confidence in myself and in the goals that I wanted to accomplish. I had no one to encourage me, inspire me and empower me. Nobody to let me know that there was a princess within me. The little girl in me needed to spread her wings in confidence, feeling protected and whole. So many areas of my life had broken pieces. Each glimpse of my past held only tainted memories. Then there were the memories that made me smile and grab hold of a little touch of hope, which lasted what seemed like a minute before the broken pieces returned, but in another way and a different path. Torn at an early age with no self-worth, no confidence and trust violated, but never knowing how and consequently left standing all alone. I needed to know that someone cared.

Before I could find my purpose, I needed to know my name. It seemed a logical impossibility to know one's destiny without first knowing one one's own identity. It was quite clear to me then, that I had to find out just who I was exactly. Not the label that society had placed on my back or the brand burned into my forehead, but who I was really was, where I belonged and who I belonged to. I needed to know that I was going to be okay standing alone. That it is possible to be alone without being lonely. After all, I was a girl that started off living in the projects with a struggling mother of five children who remarried only to find out there was dark side to her newfound husband. I didn't have the looks or the special qualities that would have allowed me to make a statement in society's eyes. We were not rich. All these issues became my private pain, my goal to pick up the broken pieces and I suppose, either accept that I wasn't ever going to fit in or find a way to fit in. Either way, I knew I'd quite likely have to be comfortable with the notion of being alone for some time.

What happens when tragedy, loss or death strikes a family? It leaves many broken pieces, guilt, anger, frustration, opinions (left unspoken or spoken) more often than not- angrily stated at the worst possible time and in the worst possible way following the provocation that such emotional chaos can bring. We even have the familiar refrains of "It's not my problem" or "Where does the responsibility lie?" the all too familiar chorus of those unwilling or unable to step up to make the tough decisions and quell the arguments that come naturally about with finances and estates up for grabs. "So whose responsibility is this?" and "Who's responsible for this?" "Somebody ought to take care of this!" Or when things become nakedly ugly, "Whose fault is this?" We now become left with unresolved issues, newly discovered after being carefully hidden away for years, inconspicuously left out of family photo albums, gingerly avoided during those awkward silences at family gatherings. It leaves cracks in the foundation of the family. Somehow the crack in the foundation soon gives way from the tremendous weight, leaving no lifeline or anchor to hold onto in order to keep the family bond strong enough to weather the storm. A storm leaves many broken pieces in its wake. The family, instead of uniting as one in strength, becomes divided by anger, resentment, envy, jealousy, blame, secret affairs, pain, hidden transgressions and the list goes on. There are accusations and arguments over "what could have been done, should have been done, what wasn't done, I was there for you time and time again while you left me twisting in the wind, you could do better or need to do better, I sacrificed everything for you, My character, integrity, self worth, only to come up empty, how could you do this and the list goes on. When we are criticized, rejected or feel that we are not good enough, it devalues our self-worth. We feel that we are not worthy. How many of us can relate to that sense of disappointment or what we feel may be betrayal in our eyes?

We are left then, with no closure and no way to understand the how and why of these difficult questions. Instead all we have left is an open casket. We can't seem to close the casket of dead issues and dry bones. We have been doing it for so long, it's all we know how to do. We're comfortable with it. And we don't know how else to operate. We have lost sight of how to move forward, how to stop looking in the rearview window of yesterday, how to stop straining our eyes to see a glimpse of our past. Sometimes, we don't feel as though we can ever move forward. To be more precise, we may feel there is no forward, nothing different from what we are experiencing, what we've experienced, and what we will experience. It was pain. It is pain. It will always be pain. It was brokenness. It will be broken and always have been brokenness. And with this refrain, we are unceasingly plagued by the questions? How do I trust again? How do I love again? How am I suppose to start over from nothing? Where do I start picking up the pieces of my life? Why did I not see this coming? Who am I? Where do I belong? Where did it all go wrong?

Our circumstances make us feel different from other people, leaving us isolated and feeling alone. We feel as though we are aliens, from another place or time, horrendously out of place and left to suffer the time traveler's plight. We feel stuck, as though our lives have been forever placed on hold. The "PAUSE" button has been pushed, as we are forced to live the life everyone else wants us to live. As a result of this, we'll end up helping everyone else, unable to help ourselves. Our good deeds for others flourishes, while our own pursuits collect dust and rot away. There, a personal war breaks out on the inside of us. We then begin to suffer in silence, starving for never having enough to nourish our very own soul after feeding those around us. Many hold positions in high places, where we are looked upon for answers from a leadership level, globally to community based, occupying offices from social, political, athletic and religious arenas. Many of our leaders have been trained in schools of business, management or government yet lack the basic foundation, which started with our teachings from home and in school. So we fall short of our expectations leaving a place of brokenness, which started long before they reached a leadership role. We hide our broken pieces in the pulpits, missionary boards, Board of Trustees, managerial and corporate positions, social gatherings from elite clubs and organizations. As a result of this, business people compromise, competitors scheme, a spirit of distrust and suspicion grows, anger and bitterness spills over into destructive life styles. Many of our community leaders lead a self-centered environment. They look out for themselves and to who or what that gets them to the next level of success. Many don't discuss the war that goes on behind closed doors of our homes and in our bedrooms. From husband and wives, to parents and children, this war spills over into violence. There is even war in our workplace between management and staff. Men abuse their wives, emotionally, physically and financially, because they feel worthless and the wives stay because they don't know their self-worth. I heard a saying "What our fathers and forefathers do in moderation, our kids do in excess." Coveting greed, "They have it and I want it at any cost." It makes me feel on the same level.

Pastors become intimidated counting the amount of members to fill their organization, leaving no room to mentor the young into great leaders for the Kingdom of God. Still holding onto the many broken pieces, yet trying to remain whole. As a result, we develop destructive attitudes and pathways trying to fix broken pieces and fill the void that we so carefully tucked away so the world can't see.

Broken pieces can leave you empty, which in turn spills over into one of the most deadly weapons that the enemy uses to entrap you into bondage. You may ask the question, "What is Bondage?" Involuntary Slavery. Bondage is dominated, restrained, by compulsion or subjugated to a controlling force or person. Especially when you are in pain. It is called "BITTER-NESS." It leaves us bleeding emotionally. Bitterness is like drinking poison. It robs you of your peace, joy and your zeal for life. It kills your spirit, which in turns drains the river of blessings to your soul. It will make you a slave to other open door weaknesses. It will paralyze your effectiveness for God and great leadership. When you choose to drink from the fountain of bitterness, you are expecting someone else to die.

How is the word that echoes through our mind the most "How do I get to that place called "peace?"

First, we must find COURAGE to step out and realize that we are here for a purpose beyond the scope of our own present understanding. We are here as players in the Divine Plan, the framework for the universe. We are not here playing by the Mine Plan, which we know exactly what happens. It hurts to heal, it hurts to find peace, it hurts to stand and be brave enough to take a stand and stand in truth and righteousness. Knowing this, no matter how bleak the situation may be, courage changes this. Courage gives us the power to be free. Free from the paths of destruction we have walked along. What's more, we are given the power to trust again, love, heal and thrive! We stop surviving life and start living life, shedding our guilt and shame and ceasing to hide the superficiality we've relied on: meaningless sex, an empty smile, designer attire and lavish suits, people that simply use us or jobs and positions that we cannot stand, but tolerate. Our Courage becomes bigger than our fears. We cease to stand in darkness and come out into the light, to stand proud as a child of God. You will stand Strong, stand Tall and stand Mighty.

You will no longer be chained to our past, but set free to run into your future fearlessly. Face your flaws, face your failures, face adversity and most of all face your pain and embrace it, rather than running from it. It has made us who we are, for better or worse, after all we are running from what God wants us to be, who we were always made and meant to be. Who we are now, who we are going to become, and who we always have been, is strong enough to take it all. After all, we have made it this far. Allow all those broken pieces, that you have gathered in your hands and allowed to manifest in your life, to be dropped. Piece by piece. All those pieces that you have held on for so long, permitting them to cut and leave scars. Piece-by-piece, give them to God. Once the shards of yesterday have been placed into the hands of a gentle, caring and loving Father, he will form a beautiful masterpiece with them. Stained glass, marred by the blood, sorrow and regret of yesterday, can create a beautiful picture today! Like a jigsaw puzzle, they will be placed back together, one piece at a time. The beauty of our father putting the pieces back together is they can never become unglued or broken. It will stand strong against the tests of time, heat, pressure, pain or destruction that tries to destroy your life. The bond becomes so strong that we will become unbreakable, as we are truly the ones that are being turned into masterpieces. You will stand out like a beautiful mosaic. Courage allows you to grow. Therein lies your key to courage.

"God is our Refuge and strength, a very present help in trouble."
~ Psalm 46:1

Step out to Step in.

We have to step out of our comfort zone. We have to hate the present state that we have been in far too long to step into your future and the things God has in store for you. We hurt people because we have been hurt. We lie to people because we have been lied to. We use, misuse and abuse people because we have been abused and misused. What we don't understand, we fear. What we fear, we fight. And what we fight, we fragment and destroy. Your pain is your promotion to what God has for you: to be greater than we ever were, are or thought we could become. Enough pain produces a desire for change, it invites us to examine our present circumstances and see what needs to be different to avoid them from becoming future circumstances as well! It invites us to know the Grace of God. You may ask what is Grace? Grace is the power that gives us the courage and the strength to stay in the fight and keep trusting God. Grace gives you that power to trust, the power to emerge triumphant, no matter what the odds against us are. You will always come out Victorious.

When Grace shines over your life, it keeps you from losing your mind. Grace rewrites our future, changes our view of the past and helps us to fully understand and appreciate our present. No matter what the severity of the mistakes, the debris of our house we worked so hard on and toiled away for hours, are not a waste, they are instead stepping stones to the future that lies before us. Grace builds us a new house. Grace opens doors that no man can shut.

This is why we must never cling to people or situations that God is trying to change. He is attempting to redirect us to greater things. He allows you to go through the pain or the situation to redirect your path. He chose us, empowered us, gave us wings to fly higher than an eagle, higher than we could ever even imagine possible. His Grace is sufficient, always enough; we can always make it through. God gives us only what he knows we can handle.

So we must let go of dead things that weight us down. Allow Grace to navigate your life. Allow

Grace to empower us and lead us on the right path of the Divine Plan. Grace clothes us while love covers us. God causes his grace toward us to be abundant. The more broken I became, the more blessed I became, not with riches, money, social status, but with Grace to stand Strong. Grace will allow you to win every battle, be the victor of every war. Even when we are at our lowest, our absolute weakest, when our frame of reference towards God is nothing but negative, even then, God's Grace is still at work.

Grace allows you to step out from behind the curtains and the shadows of your past that shroud our present and future in blindness, darkness and uncertainty.

Grace keeps you in peace when lies have been told and untrue stories remain the focus of the situation. It allows you to stand tall with godly integrity and character being at your forefront. He gives you grace to face whatever is in front of you.

Grace will equip you. God will stamp his approval on the goals that we have set and strive to reach in this lifetime.

Release it. It's time to experience Peace and Authenticity. We hold onto things even after we have gone through the mourning and grieving process. We hold on, when we should be releasing it. We become stuck. We become stuck in the Grief unable to push past the hurt. When we have lost a loved one through tragedy, disease, loss (relationships) or simply the aging process, know that, "LOVE FOLLOWS THEM."

Many times when death strikes, we spend our energy and time trying to find the reason it happened. We then start to assign death's visitation to destructive paths: "Well, he was selling drugs," "We reap what we sow" or "It's the lifestyle they were living," is the reason it happened. "Why-Why-Why? They did not deserve this!" When you release them in love, you honor the love more than the loss.

Misdiagnosing: it's the hospital's fault. My mother or father was well until they went into the hospital. They did something wrong! You gave her something to kill her or him! If you would have done what you were suppose to have done, he or she would be alive today! If you were paying close attention, this would have never happened! It's the medication that he or she was given that caused this!

We have a difficult time making peace with the situation and with the idea that just as life happens, so does death. It is something that we have no control over. We carry the guilt of "maybe if I would done something different, death would have bypassed our doorstep." "Maybe if I had...," "It's because I didn't" or "What if...? but this does nothing. We blame others when we find no PEACE. Release it and Let it Go.

We must come to the realization that we are not responsible for what has happened and have no control over death. We must release them in love and honor.

We try to avoid the grieving process. It's not the pain of losing our loved one that we really want to avoid; it's not the loss that we mourn; it's the sacred place that was once shared so close to our hearts. Treasured moments that have been robbed; sweet fantasies turned into horrible nightmares. The longing for what once was, could have been and all I could ever hoped for. It wasn't the affair I was grieving or the betrayal, but I held you close to my bosom and shared the most intimate things and moments. Heart to Heart and Soul to Soul.

He left me in this mess only to fall into the arms of another woman. The bonds of love, trust and respect have been violated. I gave you my heart with my emotions hanging on by the twist of a thread. My soul is empty. I miss the loss of how it once felt. "If I could only feel that way just one more time."

My baby was born to only be stillborn or die in her crib. "There was life inside of me." For once in my life, I felt like a complete woman. "I felt my baby's heartbeat and dance to it." For once in my life, I felt complete.

My child, I gave birth to him/her, nurtured him/her, cared for him when he was sick, school plays, PTA meetings, cheering him on at his games. It was at this time in my life that I felt whole and complete. I now have a family. One day I will have grandchildren. I have someone to love me back unconditionally. I was a part of each milestone in my child's life. I love being a parent. I wake up thinking about my child. I go to bed thinking about my child. Children are forever in our hearts. Suddenly my plans have become interrupted with the loss of one whom I once felt so close to my heart. Suddenly illness or tragedy strikes, "I am lost." "Where do I go from here?" "How did this happen and why"?

Or, maybe it's not your child. Maybe it's your parents. My parents were my rock. They have always been there for me. How do I move on? How do I get past this? I feel like the cord of life has been severed.

"I never got the chance to tell them I loved them or that I am sorry."

Grieving loss, abandonment and death is the only healing process that brings us comfort in our pain. Grief serves as an escape valve to our emotions. We must allow grief to navigate the course in our life. It's okay to grieve, but don't allow yourself to become stuck in the Why's. We must never allow negative thoughts and distorted thinking to control our thoughts. It becomes bondage when we don't seek God's help and comfort to release it. In distorted thinking, we want to get our point across in a negative way. We have even taken to social media, Facebook, Twitter, Instagram, as well as word of mouth. He said, she said, I heard or she told me to tell you, in person, text messaging, by email or by phone. There is nothing that we can do to stop loss from occurring. It's your thoughts and choices that come after the loss that counts. A broken heart is an open heart. Choose your thinking and actions wisely. Everyone has something that has happened in their life that we wish to forget. Remember "Forgetting isn't a memory lapse. It's a memory release." Let it go. Good comes out of loss, with greatness to be found. You will soon feel lighter. Peace and Glory will abound in your life.

Life comes with choices, challenges and interruptions that you never hoped to experience. Allow yourself to embrace it and go through the grieving process. The enemy will do everything he can to prey on your grief and keep you bound to it.

"Brothers and sisters, we do not want you to be uninformed about those who sleep in death, so you do not grieve like the rest of mankind, who have no hope."
~ 1 Thessalonians 4:13

Don't allow the rest of your life to be defined by the loss you've suffered. Surrender it to God!

Allow your grief to turn into your PEACE. Never get stuck in your suffering; RELEASE IT.

"Remember ye not the former things, neither consider the things of the old. Behold, I will do a new thing; now it shall spring forth; shall ye not know it? I will even make a way in the wilderness and rivers in the desert."
~ Isaiah 43: 18-19

"The prettiest smiles hide the deepest secrets, the prettiest eyes have cried the most tears and the kindest hearts have felt the most pain."
~ Anonymous

BROKEN PIECES

Broken Homes

Childhood Violations

Rape

Incest

Divorce

Abuse: Emotional, Domestic, Financial

Mistrust and Distrust

Traumatic Injuries

Loss

Diseases: Cancer, AIDS, Auto-Immune, Liver Disease

Fatherless and Motherless Daughters and Sons

Deception (He told me that he loved me so I gave in.)

Death through Unexpected Tragedy, Injuries and Diseases

Deep-Seated Fear and Guilt

Suicide or Suicide Attempts

Past Mistakes and Decisions

Grief and Disappointment

Low Self-Esteem

Dorothy Gray

Insecurity

Jealousy

Abandonment Issues

Anger Issues and Rage

Rejection

Generational Influences

Doubt and Unbelief

Unforgiveness

Negative and Pessimistic Thinking

Illicit Sexual Activity and Perversion

Drugs: Prescription Dependent to Illegal

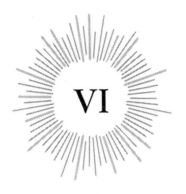

VI

Pillow Talk

"What Whispers To You In The
Midnight Hour"

As the light of the day fades away and
the hustle of our daily tasks come to a close, the in-
volvement of cooking, cleaning, shopping, work, doc-
tor's visits and such, there is one thing that we are not
in competition with, or should I say compete with,
and that is "PILLOW TALK."

As we rest our aching bodies and exhausted
minds on our soft pillows after pushing ourselves to

the very edge of our limits during the course of the day, which can be from a work day of eight hours or more, a sleepless night waiting for a loved one to call or return home safely or any other way a day is made up. Our mind and soul becomes a battlefield of emotions that are allowed to run free, becoming a raucous spiral that whirls even faster out of control until we can't hear our heartbeat. As we lay our tired head down on our soft pillows, our bed has become our own private island that holds no boundaries, against or over our past pain or present issues that we are wrestling with. It becomes a reflection of all the feelings that have seeped into our minds throughout the day, weeks, months or even years, better yet, our past. We find ourselves in a reflection of our emotions and what we are dealing with: good, bad, happy and sad. We look for answers to life's simplest tasks, questions and a light to help us see.

Who calls your name when the lights are out and the room is dark and the night is still? There is no one to talk to but ourselves, our thoughts incessantly, relentlessly, replaying over and over again, like looking at a reflection of ourselves in a House of Mirrors. All our fears, issues, hang-ups and private affairs seem to appear on our own deserted island, which we came to in order to escape it all. Anger, pain, deception, lies, mistakes, old loves, new loves, childhood pain, violations, rage, bitterness, change, unresolved issues, loss through divorce or death, loose ends that we have yet to find any peace with; the list goes on through the night.

As we lay our heads on our soft pillow, we sometimes cover our faces, looking for comfort. We might even allow the tears to flow. Often we are a captive audience, watching old movies in our mind of the most private and intimate times that we never share with anyone, moments that we are too embarrassed to talk about, let alone admit, and yes, even the darkest, unlabelled tapes that contain our biggest mistakes, regrets, conflicts and pain. They remain stashed away in our mind, blanketed with dust, buried in a dark corner, tucked away in a nondescript box that we hoped to never find again. Yet, we have held on to them all the same. Sadly, our memories are not as fragile as home videos.

So we look for comfort and solace in Pillow Talk. We allow our minds to roam free, even in the most desolate places we've wandered through hundreds of times before, desperately searching for peace. Whatever I give a voice to in Pillow Talk, that is what shows up. It whispered to me. Whatever I give a voice to in Pillow Talk, whatever I allow and entertain, is what soon haunts me. It adds to it a symphony of events that play over and over. All those private issues cause us to raise this wall around our hearts, leaving us with nowhere to run. The callousness that I have allowed to become hardened over my heart to protect myself from the hurt and the pain of being myself has left me incarcerated. It has left me with nowhere to run. So I become at war with myself trying to find peace for my weary soul. These issues that we so desperately attempt in vain to bury, torments and robs us of our serenity. It has robbed us of our rightful place called PEACE, as well as a good night sleep. They rob us of feeling that we are safe.

Our security becomes stolen from us by these private issues that we choose to ignore or try our hardest to pretend they simply don't exist. All those private issues that we chose not to deal with soon becomes an escalade of our lives, which sooner or later becomes open and public so all the world can see. We step over into unfamiliar territory that we have no knowledge or understanding of in the slightest. All those private issues and secret sins we choose not to deal with soon become public in one form or the other.

Throughout our life's journey, we will experience things that break us down to the point that it breaks us open. And in that breaking open, we uncover things that were lying dormant. It causes us to leak issues that can open us up to weaknesses. It's once we are starting to break open, with nobody else to talk to, that we began to Pillow Talk. At night, all this surfaces on our own private island of emotions. Wounds from the past, present circumstances and anticipation of our future pain.

As a little girl growing up in the projects, my Momma, a single parent of five children, divorced, no college education, only what life could teach her, and left alone to fend for herself. She had grown up without a foundation or manual to direct her along the pathways of life. Especially with all the curveballs and detours that life throws at you. Momma's biological mother died when she was in diapers. During the day, Momma was full of joy, talking to friends, neighbors or family about current events, the weather or her latest shopping excursions. All appeared normal and no different from everyone else on the outside. During the day, Momma had it all together relishing the joy she felt while being in the company of others. It was in the quiet and stillness of the night that Momma was left alone in her pain, alone in Pillow Talk. On particularly restless nights, Momma would rise from bed and vigorously clean the house in a vain attempt to also scrub the blood from and heal the pain in her soul. She would clean until she was too tired to do anything else but sleep. Momma did her best to not wake us, an effort that proved futile. How could we not hear the record player was blasting? The record player would blast medicine for her soul in the early morning hours while she sang to it. One in particular that gave her serenity, for I would hear it many nights, was "Where is Your Faith?" by James Cleveland. Perhaps it was a sort of torment, wondering aloud, what happened, and how she could get back on the right track. Then, there were nights that you could hear various artists from her era, James brown, Otis Redding, Gladys Knight and the Pips and the list goes on. There were times she would search, seemingly to no avail, for the right prescription; nights where even this too failed and the sounds of music were replaced with cries. These were the nights that the music could not bring her the comfort and peace that she needed.

I would awaken at midnight to hear Momma crying and wonder as any little girl would, "What was going on?" "Momma what's wrong?" I was always a curious girl, asking questions. "Why are you crying in the late night hours? During the day, you seem so happy."

Too young to understand life, too young to even begin to comprehend what Momma was facing, I thought I was old enough to help her figure it out. She was pushing through all those emotional tidal waves that are impossible to survive alone. She was dealing with all those emotional undercurrents that seemed too hard to bear alone. Momma never learned as a young woman how to navigate the waters of her life. Her fears, guilt, shame, mistakes, sorrow, anger, unanswered questions, regrets and past pain were all things she either did not talk about growing up in the immediate family or too afraid to talk about it.

Feelings aren't as important as when and where the next meal will come. Needless to say, she desperately needed closure in certain chapters of her life, something to put these things to rest. There was no guidebook to show her how to get to the next chapter. So, at night her bed became her private island, holding no boundaries.

The bridge to tomorrow had not yet been built, for she was still trying to clean up the destruction of yesterday. At night, her bed became her private island, home to everything she brought to it. It was the cries from Momma's room that made me realize she has been dealing with pitfalls, heartbreaks, disappointments and closure to certain chapters of her life that were left open with no answers to bring closure to move forward. After all, how could she move forward when she had no understanding of her past? She was reliving the pain of yesterday. Each time a crisis arose, when there was a dilemma on her hands, every time she was in some way reminded her of the pain, it became a trigger point to the pressure zone. There was no one for Momma to talk to in the midnight hour. Momma had no one to encourage, empower or inspire her, or offer one word that could change her destiny. She had no one to tell her to keep pushing through her pain. Momma was looking for answers to the questions that had been responded to with "NOTHING" for so long. The response was empty. Momma was looking for the missing pieces of her life. What was plaguing her soul behind those closed doors and her private island? Loneliness, brokenness, broken marriage, self-worth, fighting through present day circumstances, emotional abuse, physical abuse, missing pieces, broken pieces, feeling unaccepted to fit in. The little girl in her that never got a chance to just laugh, breathe in life and to exhale all her fears, to feel loved and protected. She was that little girl that was never held in her breaking. Momma became stuck in the shadows of her pain. Her bed became her private island and the pillow was her solace to shed her tears. I would stay awake to talk to her, so she could just feel better for morning. After all, the sun would rise soon and she with it.

There were nights I found myself sitting on the floor right in front of her, yet impossibly far away all the same. Some nights as the tears flowed down her face and her emotions burst forth as if from a broken dam that finally gave up and was no longer able to hold back her wounds, shortcomings, her pitfalls, heartbreaks, let downs and, more than anything, unanswered questions that flooded the room and most of all flooded my mind, a curious little girl that just didn't understand life, but to just be a listener. Unanswered questions are the worst, for they unceasingly torment us, sometimes as whispers, but most often as screams. And so it was with Momma. When unanswered questions are left unresolved with no closure, they continue to be your silent whispers of the night. There was a gaping hole left in her soul that never was mended. Her pillow became her comfort zone and her bed became her private island, the island of her past. After all, how could she (how could any-one?) expect to move forward with her present and into her exciting future when she was struggling to comprehend her densely painful past, in order to be able to release it? She had no understanding of her past. There I sat, as one moment as she was talking and the next crying, not as her daughter, the curious and confused little girl with no understanding of life, but as her counselor. All I had been taught, all I knew how to do, was pray that somehow she would be okay. Somehow she would find a way to be at peace with childhood trauma, the physical and verbal abuse that plagued her memory for so long; the chains of her pain that were holding her tightly in bondage needed to be broken.

Then one night, after a tiring day, I fell asleep from exhaustion. I awoke to find that my mother had been rushed to the hospital in the middle of the night from a hemorrhage. She'd been hemorrhaging. Fear gripped my heart the way a child clings to her mother. Now the roles have switched. I have now gone from being a listener and a counselor for Momma, to a scared, confused and curious little girl, the way I wished I could hold my mother at that very moment. The grief, confusion and the pain hit me like a giant boulder. My four siblings and I were hurled off to stay with my aunt until we were told otherwise. So there we were, waiting, steeping in our uncertainty. Day after day, week after week and still no answer about Momma's condition. No phone to call her. Momma, just let me hear your voice. All I wanted to know and needed to know, "Are you okay?" Those weeks of not knowing, not hearing, seemed to be eternities. Still, no answer.

Many felt that I was too young to understand. So in the late night hour and the stillness of the night, where day and night both melt away into some netherworld, as we focus on what plagues us, it was there that I began to Pillow Talk. At that moment, my mother's fate was uncertain. What happened? What was her condition now and was she going to be all right? All these questions became the base of my island, one with razor wire instead of sand. Yet, somehow, my pillow was my comfort. I couldn't wait till the late night hour to lay my head against the pillow and just let the tears flow. If I lost Momma, my world would be shattered. So, as I waited impatiently for weeks, it was to my pillow that I would take my tears and my sorrow, without judgment or any interruptions. The harder I held the pillow, the more the tears would flow. It became my silent comforter in my time of pain, allowing me to feel.

It was my pillow that showed me solace, when no one was able to hold and comfort me, talk to me or even just say to me, true or not, knowing or unknowing, everything would be okay.

It was my pillow that let me know I could rise up and know that a new day is here. It was time for me to rise up and face it.

FINDING STRENGTH IN BROKEN PLACES

It was my pillow that taught me quiet strength.

It was my pillow that allowed me to examine my feelings and discard what had no logical basis. I could filter out all the impurities that were flooding my thoughts and emotions at a young age.

It was my pillow that accepted all of my frustrations and anger.

It was my pillow that silenced my fear.

It was my pillow that helped me find a happy place and grab a firm hold of hope. After all, hope and faith was all I had to hold on to!

And so, yes, it was indeed my pillow too, that taught me about God, about prayer and about Faith. I learned at an early age how to pray. I'd always heard talk about God, but who was this big God? I needed to find God! I needed this God to heal my mother. I need you God to show thyself to me, strong and mighty. After all, who was I? A confused and curious little girl from the projects with so much determination and yet destined to try and figure things out.

Weeks later, my aunt came forth with word on my mother, finally! She was going to be all right. She would be coming home soon, but she would have to remain on strict bed rest. God heard the cries of a scared little girl and the prayers of many that were praying for her. Upon Momma's return home from the hospital, there was something different about her. Something happened while Momma was in the hospital. Now there was a bible that never left her bedside. Now, in the dark, still, cold night, I no longer heard her weeping, singing or cleaning to escape her pain, but praying. In the midnight hour, a light of a decidedly different kind filled her room and I saw her reading her bible. No longer did I hear the cries of pain, but cries of Praise. No longer did I hear the record player blasting as a cry for peace and comfort, but I could hear the words of thanksgiving and supplication. She was at peace and walking in peace. I no longer heard the cries of defeat, but the spirit of survival. The prescription to her painful past, which caused her to walk with a limp, became her bible that held the key to her walking victoriously into her future. No longer will she be able to allow her struggles, self-worth, fear and a tainted past to cause her to walk with her head held down, but to walk into something new called the newness of life and wholeness. Her prescription became the Word of God.

He spoke to her storms, "Peace be still." (Mark 4:39)

He spoke to her brokenness, "The Lord is near to the brokenhearted. And saves those who are crushed in spirit." (Psalm 34:18)

He spoke to her fears, "Perfect love casts out all fears." (1 John 4:18) She began to allow her past to pass over her like the waters moving in the sea. Deliverance was becoming the brand that made those rough places smooth and the crooked places straight.

He spoke of restoration and brought life back into her body, "Heal me, oh Lord and I shall be healed, save me and I shall be saved, for you are my praise." (Jeremiah 17:14)

"Lord my god, I cried out to you and you healed me. O Lord, you brought my soul up from the grave; you have kept me alive, that I should not go down to the pit." (Psalm 30: 2-3)

"Oh Lord, I cried out to you and you healed me." (Psalm 30:2)

He spoke to her self-esteem and her self-worth, "But the Lord said to Samuel, "Do not consider his appearance or his height, for I have rejected him. The Lord does not look at the things people look at. People look at the outward appearance, but the Lord looks at the heart." (1 Samuel 16:7)

"Therefore, if any man be in Christ, he is a new creature: old things are passed away; behold, all things are become new." (2 Corinthians 5:17)

"For I know the plans I have for you, declares the Lord, "plans to prosper you and not to harm you, plans to give you hope and a future." (Jeremiah 29:11)

And so, it is abundantly clear then, that as we begin to at last relinquish all of the pain that drove us to our pillows in sorrow. For days, weeks, months or even years, we now have a place that we can release them into. "It is the arms of a Gentle and Loving God." This was spoken by Isaiah 10:27, "And it shall come to pass in that day, that his burden shall be taken away from off thy shoulder and his yoke from off thy neck and the yoke will be destroyed because of the anointing." He releases an anointing."

Some may ask what is the anointing? The anointing spoken of is the Power of God, God's blessing over us that protects and covers us. It illuminates our pathways and us. It brings divine order into our lives. "Let all things be done decently and in order." (1 Cor. 14:40) Wisdom and Favor will flow in your life and over your life like unstoppable currents. He will not leave us without comfort. No, rather, he will instead release us from the trapdoor of bondage and captivity, to open doors to experience him like no other in the midnight hour. The anointing breaks yokes. (A yoke is something that places the destiny of a man in the hands of the enemy.) The anointing, teaches you, guides, protects and empowers you. When the anointing comes, light exposes darkness, and truth exposes a lie. The anointing attracts some people into your life and often will alienate others. As you begin to obey the Holy Spirit and seek after the things of God, many will withdraw from you. You will find yourself, all by yourself in his presence. Where his presence is, your weaknesses will die out and strength will abound in your life. Whatever you are facing in life, from trials to tribulations, hardships, divorce, loss or anything beyond your control, know that you are anointed to face it, to overcome it, to restore it and transform it. You are anointed for VICTORY. For, he enjoys your companionship.

"Blessed is the man whose strength is in thee: in whose heart are the ways of them. Who, passing through the valley of Baca, makes it a well. The rain also filleth the pools. They go from strength to strength." This is where you will experience the fragrance of his presence and true peace. You will soon arise with a spirit of thanksgiving and with a heart of praise."

~ Psalm 85: 5-7

VII

Secrets

Generations of Secrets and Lies Create Chaos and Confusion

As we go through the chaos of varying degrees that is our daily existence in our different professions, from blue collar to white Collar, we walk around holding tightly to whispered words and remembered promises. Some of us are stay at home moms and dads, while the rest may be working to help provide for the family. At the close of the day, we so hurriedly come home to have our dinner and rest our tired bodies to plan for another day. It is one thing that we may never talk about. But when pain is involved, it becomes a different story. It is behind closed doors, in hushed tones so as not to be over-heard, that we can become transparent and talk about it. Or there can be so much pain involved that we don't ever talk about it. Many times when we have become conditioned by being told by our parents or other family in authority roles: "What goes on in this house stays in this house. It didn't happen the way it was told. Now you have Blown this situation out of Proportion. You must not tell anyone. It will bring embarrassment to the family name. We can talk about this later or You're just trying to tear the family apart.

We look upon Secrets then as insignificant, something "all in our head." I have been fortunate enough to connect with different people to hear the stories of their pain. From a myriad of backgrounds, they have trusted me enough to be transparent with things that have happened in their life, even those behind closed doors. As I am sitting and listening to their stories, I too feel like a loaded gun with my hand on the trigger ready to explode from the pain. I too learned that I was not alone. I so needed to be transparent and allow God to bring a healing balm to my situation so I can be whole, free, transparent, and most of all, have a platform to tell my story. As I am sitting and talking with them, I begin to notice their demeanor and their body language began to shift as we began to talk about certain areas of their life or certain people. I soon realized that in order to help them bring healing, wholeness and closure, I needed to get to the heart of the matter. I needed to reach to the core of the soul.

I often think of the situation that I had a year ago when I noticed a bump on my neck the size of a pea. Many did not notice the area but I began to pay more attention to it, maybe out of annoyance or out of paranoia that others would soon start to take notice of it. I noticed over a period of time it started to become larger. The larger it became, the more tender to the touch it was starting to become. Again, here I was worried that others would notice, as it was becoming larger. So I decided to try home remedies, hoping that it would go away on its own. It continued in spite of these efforts to become larger and increasingly painful and tender to touch. So I tried hiding it behind turtle neck sweaters and concealed makeup. My greatest fear was I would have this large scar on the side of my neck. Having tried everything though, I knew I could not hide it any longer and it had to be dealt with. So I decided to fly back to Florida for an appointment with the dermatologist. Once the dermatologist came into the examining room, he made a decision that it was a large cyst that can be excised right in the office with a local anesthetic. This was the furthest thing from my radar at that moment. I was more afraid of what people would think, like "Perceptions of Exposed Se-crets," than dealing with the problem. He was able to excise the cyst, which turned out to be larger than expected to be. He then packed the area with gauze and sent me home. While driving home, I noticed my shirt was soaked with blood. I then rushed home and immediately started to apply direct pressure to the wound to try and stop the bleeding. After thirty minutes and still unable to stop the bleeding, I drove myself to the hospital with one hand on the steering wheel and the other hand applying pressure to my neck. After arriving at the Emergency Room, I was escorted immediately back to one of the rooms. There, the Nursing staff attempted to stop the bleeding by applying more pressure to try and stop the bleeding, but to no avail. So the next step was to obtain a CAT Scan to try and find out where the bleeding was coming from. So it is with our Emotional pain. Before we can be healed or receive a healing, we must first stop the bleeding. You can't treat an open wound if it is bleeding. With emotional pain, we have to address the Emotional pain, then work on the underlying issues. Many times in life we delay the process by avoiding the situation until there comes a point in time that it must be dealt with so we can move forward in our lives, until we start uncontrollably. When we become wounded, we need to treat the wound immediately and deal with it. The same thing had been going on with my neck. Hoping that it was just a small bump underneath the skin and would go away on its own. I chose not to deal with it, telling myself there was nothing to worry about. The next thing we must do is move to the core of what is causing the emotional pain. "Where is the first initial Breakdown?" After two hours and multiple needle sticks to insert a large bore needle for IV Contrast, the CAT Scan was still not able to trace where the bleeding was coming from. Suddenly the bleeding finally stopped and the wound sealed itself. I called it God's grace. There was no nick found in the carotid artery. Yet it left me needing to remain careful in the days to come not to add trauma, heavy-lifting or anything that may cause the area to bleed again or the wound to not heal effectively. It is the same with Emotional Pain, healing is starting to take place, we must be careful to not add anymore trauma to the area and drama to your life.

When a crisis is thrust upon us, we must be careful not to panic and create trigger points for ourselves, opening us up to further pain or paths of destruction. We have to feel protected and safe. For the first 24 hours my neck was bruised, swollen and very noticeable with a large bandage placed on it. There are painful and tender areas that need to be protected, until we see that those areas of our lives are healed. Once the bandage is removed and the area is healed, we are left with a scar. Some scars are larger than others and some are deeper than others. The larger and deeper the scar, the more time it takes for the scar to fade away. The greater the pain is, the more time it takes us to heal. Sadly those are less prone to fading the same way that scars are!

During the healing process, we must focus our time on nurturing, protecting, caring and taking small steps until we are again able to take the bigger steps, able to run and fly once more. It is vital that we steer clear of the paths that are filled with triggers. We must avoid these trigger points that can cause setbacks and flare up. This emotional roller coaster ride creates an entry point for weaknesses; weakness allows an entry point for Demonic Spirits, which can then take over your life. It invariably leaves us tremendously exhausted and weak after even just one ride. (How much more defeated are we then, on the fifth-time around). Once they start to work in your life, no matter how tiny the crack in the window is, they will come with full force, sabotaging everything, working relentlessly to destroy your life. One of these weaknesses an entity will exploit is Secrets. Sin, Pain and Secrets, like dirt swept under a rug, do not disappear. When covered up and ignored, they never heal. These three forces (sin, pain, secrets) like rust, wear away at our soul until we are destroyed.

"The thief cometh not, but to steal and to kill and to destroy. I am come that they

might have life and they might have it more abundantly."

~ John 10:10

When you have generations of secrets and lies within the family, it creates generations of chaos and confusion. It leaves unanswered questions and trust is nowhere to be found. Those secrets were allowed to fester for years between generations. It leaves us with unanswered questions and trust issues. It soon begun to erode the foundation of the family. Family trust becomes compromised, especially when the secret becomes compromised by a lie and hidden from family members. Family trust gets lost in the wind, lost in the den of a secret discovered by a lie exposed, after hiding in plain sight for years. Once the trust is broken, division in the family takes center stage. We soon start to take sides. We all try to convince the "others" that we are right and that they ought to see it from their eyes. Family members take sides with the member who can convince the others that he or she is the one who has proven his or her case and the others should see the story from his or her standpoint. Different ideas about what is best for the family, what will bring healing, what the truth is and how to deal with the betrayal, all create a whirlwind of grief and drama. This can continue for years, leaving some family members merely as names spoken about, in hushed tones.

Family secrets help operate an addiction, with each family member playing a role. When the secret is no longer a secret, Healing can take place, once the initial shock and sense of betrayal are properly moved through. When healing starts to take place, you give it light with room to breathe. Truth steps in and reigns over the situation. We then allow ourselves to know who we are and our position within the family dynamics. When family secrets break down the trust, it soon becomes a play acted out on the center stage of each of our lives, then passed down to each generation, if not healed or broken. When not healed, family drama starts the process called erosion. Drama turns to decay. As the family secret continues to fester, it continues to erode the family foundation. As the secret continues to devour the family, trust is an ever-growing fantasy. For there is no trust with lies kept tucked away for years. This is when the game of pretend begins. We go to the ends of the earth to maintain the facade that we are living the picture perfect life with an unbreakable family bond. What of truth? It will come out. It always does. "If it don't catch you in the wash. Lord knows it'll catch you in the rinse."

Secrets may come out in physical symptoms, resulting in stress and guilt for the person carrying the knowledge. It may come out in chronic aches and pain, severe headaches, stomach issues, skin conditions from rashes to sudden breakouts over the body, depression, suicidal ideations, anxiety, panic attacks, Behavioral problems and the list goes on. Sooner or later addictions and addictive behavior, compulsive shopping or gambling, sexual promiscuity, substance abuse (drugs and alcohol) comes in to play, especially if the secrets have been buried for long periods of time, bringing a sense of betrayal, shame, guilt to such a level that some cannot deal with it. They blame themselves. As we continue to role-play for long periods of time, paranoia starts to take center stage. We then become emotionally territorial.

When you have secrets in the family, they protect the family and their dignity or the dignity of the person whose sin society would frown upon. Their sin has been kept shrouded in secrecy. Pride and ego combine with secrets have become a recipe for hurt and continuous cover-ups. It leads to a constant cycle of hushing things up, until someone gets sick of hiding behind the secret and wants to be free.

As a little girl growing up, I missed and longed for my Biological father. I longed for him so much that at times I found myself aching. Yet all the same, my mother remarried. He was a man, prior to the union, who was attentive, caring, hard working, great provider and a motivated businessman with two successful businesses. Momma thought that he would be a great father, a man that was willing to take on five kids and raise us as his own. Soon we were a blended family with a different home. A new home out of the projects, new cars, money in the bank and successful businesses. Momma was happy for once in her life. She would not have to struggle. We enjoyed the holiday gatherings, vacations, family reunions, the picture perfect American family. If he returned home early from work and Mom was working late, he would start the evening meals. After we became settled in new schools, with new friends from the neighborhood, we experienced all the peace and happiness this new life offered.

What my mother didn't realize, and what she did not see, is the man who helped her find happiness and made her feel safe had a dark side to him. He had a box of secrets he was carefully hiding away with secret sins.

One night, Momma was working late. Sometimes her job would require her to stay overnight. My stepfather made an attempt to violate me. There I was this small framed girl fighting like I never had before. Fighting for my innocence, for my life. This night felt like my darkest hour. In the aftermath, I was utterly at a loss for words, riddled with confusion, terror frightened as the dream turned to a nightmare. I felt as if I was having a breakdown mentally and physically. I felt as if my legs could not hold my small body and they would just give way any minute. But I had to fight. Fortunately, Grace had me covered. Needless to say, sleep did not come to me that horrid night and neither did the help I so desperately needed. I needed to stay strong. The light of the day saw me cold and despondent for lack of sleep and a shattered heart. My mind had become like a ship without a sail, with a welter of emotions running rampant. Momma, I need you to come and rescue me from this pain. At last, morning came. As Momma pulls into the driveway, from the look on my face, she knew something was terribly wrong. There I sat inside the car telling her what happened. After I told her, we both entered the house together, there Momma confronted him. His response was simply "silence." The room became very cold.

After the confrontation, Momma held me close and told me that she loved me and to be strong. At that moment in my life, how could I be strong, when I felt so confused and weak? Not knowing what to do next, the day schedule continues on as planned. School. Momma decided to drive me to school. As we got a quarter mile from home, I notice her body language begun to change. Momma could not hold back the tears. "Momma what's wrong?" "What's wrong?" Now I am hurting more because Momma is crying. Confused, worried that I'd done something wrong, I sat silently hating myself. Maybe I should have remained silent. Momma, please don't cry. Momma at that point pulled over to wipe the tears from her eyes that could not stop flowing. There she began to tell me of some things that happened to her as a little girl. She bore deep emotional hurts, which she suffered in silence for many years. So I found myself then, back in that familiar place, there with my mother having to be that emotional rock for her to lean on. Never mind the support I needed. At that point her world was shattered and her trust had been violated. While I needed understanding of all this, I also recognized I needed to comfort my mother. But how can a child comfort her mother when she barely understands it all herself. To help Momma find peace and make sense of everything, there was my godmother Dorothy whom I was named after. My godmother became that pillar of strength and that strong tower of prayer that held the bond together between Momma and me so we could get through this. I needed peace for my soul and I needed to breathe. Momma needed strength and guidance.

One month had gone by and things seemed to have returned to normal in the house. As for me, still dreadfully confused and emotionally guarded in a way no child should ever have to be. I learned then how to pretend. The emotional pain was excruciating, but I knew I had to pretend to be happy. I learn how to role-play. Because of this I never got closure. Once during a holiday gathering, I was asked to step into the kitchen by my mother. No one was around other than my mother and he. There he wanted to apologize for his behavior. I accepted his apology but at the same time, how can one apologize for such an act? And most important "Did it come from the heart?" Yet with the formalities taken care of, the secret was quietly ignored.

The family secret was locked away, in order to protect my stepfather's dignity. The cycle of the secret had only just begun. Although the apology was accepted, little did I know the fire was just starting to burn. I had two other sibling sisters; neither have the same biological father as me. It was then the physical traits (my skin color in particular) that differentiated me from them mattered. When it was time for family vacations, I was not allowed to go. Momma was told there would not be enough room in the car for me. "She needs to go stay with someone," he said. There were portraits that I was not a participant. "She is too dark," in other words too black. Momma became a silent participant in an unhealthy situation to keep the peace within the family while I suffered in silence, confused and full of pain. Many times I wanted Momma to be happy with my accomplishments and the goals that I had started to pursue, which she could not be happy. She didn't know how to be happy, because no one else was happy. There I was confused, wanting to feel accepted, low self-esteem and wanting to know that I mattered. Can someone please tell me where do I belong? And whom do I belong to?

So while the vacations and family reunions went on, I was left to stay with my godmother. With godmother, I felt at peace. She knew my story and loved me all the same. There were nights I would sleep next to her feeling whole, accepted and most of all loved. While she rose early in the morning to pray, wash and clean the house, goddaddy would be in the kitchen cooking with aroma of fish and grits wafting throughout the house from the kitchen before tending to his garden. It was at godmother's house that I finally felt accepted with a sense of belonging. After all god-momma knew my story. It was her love and praying for me is where I found strength and refuge. Before leaving godmother's home to return back to home, she would always make it clear to me that "she loved me and I could call her anytime." But I felt it wasn't enough.

There I would have to return home. Again, the fire is slowly burning and the malevolent malfunctioning slowly taking center stage again. Many times when he would arrive home, the tone of the room was set on how he was feeling. He set the stage on the spirit of the household. (Have you ever received an invitation to a person's home or an outing when a certain person would show up and the entire spirit of the room would shift by just the presence of that person- be it positive energy or negative energy?) Pain was his name with anger written all over his face. The more silent Momma became, the more control my stepfather maintained in making decisions that I was not allowed to be a part of. This was his way of punishing me. There I was, a broken spirit in so many ways. So I learned how to mask my emotions, becoming a chameleon, appearing numb to my circumstances, while all the while fighting to be free. Free in the knowledge that "I am not responsible for adult actions." "Free to release the Pain that looks me back in the mirror." "Free to release the guilt of what I was feeling "thinking look what I have created." "Free to know that I spoke in Truth. It was truth that broke the chain of sin and the curse that would have cost me my life, joy, bitter memories and choosing wrong paths in search of the wrong kind of love. Most of all

"Free to know that I was Loved, Loveable, Loving and accepted as I was."

So I would lock myself away in my room, hiding there, in the only safe place I could find. Here in this haven, sanctuary, I could escape the pain and the uncomfortable feeling I would experience when I would have to see him. My room was where I could escape the turmoil and take my mind to a happy place. I felt as if I had an elephant strapped to my back, that I was forced to carry alone. I never got true closure. Again, his dignity continued to be protected and I had to endure the consequences of his stroked ego. Momma was still overwhelmed, consumed by these dark frailties.

As the years went by, I soon learned that my stepfather grew up in a house full of family secrets, secret sins and pain that was hidden away, but all the same accepted as normal. "Just the way things are." Generations of secrets, sin and lies always create generations and the generations to come of chaos. Soon all those private issues that we so carefully tucked away or chose not to deal with show up and turn into a public mayhem. It becomes our public pain. All those secrets that we held close to our heart, the conversations we said we didn't have, sequences of events that we say never happened; it all begins to torment us. Years of pain finds its way into the lives of our children, which in turn connects to their children, creating a generation of strongholds and bondage. "What our fathers and forefathers have done in moderation, our children do in excess." This has become our acceptance speech. The door to sin has been opened and the excuses become truths we accept, as we know no other way. Soon we find ourselves dealing with generational curses. We inherit a susceptibility to sin in areas that troubled our forefathers. Momma never learned how to navigate the waters of her fears. As a little girl growing up, she never had someone to speak into her life and over her life. This all reminds me of the Bible story that speaks of Ruth growing up in a land of Incest and Sin. She never had anyone to guide her through her life until she met Naomi and so Naomi's God became her God.

My mother didn't have a Naomi, though. Instead, Momma only knew Physical and Verbal abuse at the hands of her stepmother. That was one of the first initial breakdowns in her life. This was one of the things that was never brought to the table and dealt with, so healing and forgiveness can be written on her heart. She didn't get that, so her heart remained locked in the past. She was unable to grow up, to learn emotional and spiritual maturity. We all have come from something, even our parents. So the question lies in us. What do we do then seeing our scars exposed? And, where does that leave us?

Well, it is important not to become our parent's and grandparent's tragedies. We no longer have to become enslaved to yesterday's pain or the things that have held us captive and in bondage, we know how far it can go and the end results. We know that it only perpetuates in perpetuity unless it is resolved.

It is the pain of yesterday that can hold us in captivity and keeps us from realizing our goals and dreams. It prevents us from moving forward. But once we are able to move forward and let go, we can come to a place of not reaching back to our past. We can finally let go of the "WHY" and cease to drive ourselves in a futile attempt to figure it all out. "Why did it happen?" What should have been, but never did.

So to find that love that I was longing for, I set sail on a journey to find my biological father, not knowing where to start. "Daddy, I just need to find you. Daddy, do you love me? Daddy, I need you to tell me just who I am. Daddy, why did you go?" I was determined to find my father. "Daddy, I need you now." Each night I would lie in bed and pray for God to bring Daddy back to me. There I was, a little girl with big Faith to believe that God was going to answer my prayer. I needed him. After all, everyone said I looked just like you, except a little darker complexion. I needed someone to help me to make sense of it all. To hold me and tell me everything would be okay.

One day, six months later, as I am skimming through the newspaper while sitting in my room, a picture caught my eye. It was my Dad!" A photographer had photographed him one afternoon returning from work. There was no mistaking what lay before me. I felt that God had at last shined a light so bright down on me, to let me know that everything would be all right. There I was, jumping for joy, excited that I found Daddy. I couldn't wait any longer, I had to call my oldest Brother and share the news. "Guess what? I found Daddy!" He was happy also. My oldest brother and I had a strong bond, always doing what he could to protect me. So we took it upon ourselves to see if we could find where this picture was taken. My brother had just gotten his driver's license. One afternoon we decided to find the place where the photograph was taken. So we started on a dark road, mapping out the location of the picture. Our hunt led us to a convenience store. We then ask the cashier did he recognize the man in the picture. Hesitantly, he was curious what we wanted with this stranger. When we told him we were sure we'd discovered our father, he told us where we could find him. The cashier looked excited and proceeded to tell us where we could find Daddy. My brother and I drove up to the home where Dad was living. As we started to get out of the car, a man yelled into the house for my Dad. "There are people out here looking for you." There, we took one look at Daddy with the biggest smile on his face. I felt that God had just shined the brightest light into my world. There, we sat for hours soaking in Daddy's presence and caught up on what was happening in our everyday life, school and part-time jobs. We weren't looking for material possessions or money. The greatest gift we were looking for was hearing Daddy say "I love you." There were no questions as to why he left us or what he didn't do, or could have done. We just wanted to feel the love of Daddy and know that he was okay. One year later,

Daddy decided to move closer to us. There was never a weekend or holiday that had gone by that we did not spend with our father. Years of missing and longing for Daddy seemed like it was only yesterday.

"There is a free spirit and a true
spirit within each of us

it is the combination of both our
free spirit and true spirit

"that enables us to discover the
mysteries of the our soul."

~ Deanna Blesser

VIII

Push It Back

The rain had been pounding the concrete all day, but all the same, I wanted to enjoy some fresh air, so I decided to sit on my back porch. There I sat, looking out at my yard, being thankful for all I had and all I'd given to get where I was... But as I stood up to walk back inside, I found myself taking note of my neighbor's yards around me. I noticed my home was sitting lower than others. When the skies would open up and torrential rains would come, it was my yard that would flood. I would get the overflow of water and debris from each neighbor's yard and was then left to clean up the mess.

Upon reflection, I sought counsel from a professional in order to resolve the issue, who advised me to build up my back yard, focusing on all those low lying areas that were causing me to retain the debris and excess water. Ready and willing to fix an issue that I hadn't noticed (or perhaps forgotten about), I signed off on the project and so along came the truck of fill dirt. That was just the start of the project. I knew that I would have to put a lot of work in to fix what was allowed to accumulate and fester over the years. So I hired a landscaper to get rid of all the weeds and till the remaining dirt. Once the existing dirt is turned over, new fill dirt can be added and the dirt can be graded. Once the grading of the old and new dirt is finished and the new foundation is built strong, sturdy, stable and is able to handle the debris that before led to the problems, then something new can begin, something beautiful. But that new beginning can only happen if we take our existing circumstances, our present pain and give it up. We have to first turn it over.

Too often in life, we have allowed people to dump their issues, opinions, judgments and pain into our lives. We have allowed family to saturate and bound us with their wrong choices and their destructive pathways they have chosen. We take their criticism, carry their hurt and hold their secrets, leaving us with guilt, either out of fear, the inability to say No. That additional load can be impossible to bear if we cannot even manage our own lives! But we don't turn away, we don't say no, even when we know what it does to us. Part of our healing, turning things over, pushing back the pain, is owning our power. We need to learn when we are able to help others and when we are not. Further, we need to know if we are helping too much or not. We cannot (and should not even begin to try!) to control others. After all, we've likely been (intentional or accidental) victim of that same kind of behavior. When we turn it over, we also are turning over these unhealthy patterns we've learned.

Yes, with healing comes discernment on who to help and how and more importantly, it comes with a laser focus of self-care. This means not walking into snares and entrapments, not taking abuse and not taking care of someone that doesn't need it. (Caretaking is different from helping. Caretaking is the act of doing things for others when they are fully capable of doing it themselves (often to the detriment of the helper!) This is why forms of emotional escape, or passions such as creative expression, or exercise, or anything we choose to do to "get away from it all" are important. They are acts of self-care. Letting go and doing what is best for ourselves. This does not mean we cease to be compassionate, but we have to know when to let go, no matter how much we may love those who try and put themselves on us.

Far too long, we have allowed family to saturate and bound us with their wrong choices and destructive pathways that they have chosen, leaving us with the guilt either out of fear, the inability to say No, or a family system that's been set in place, commonly called dysfunctional family. Do not be put off by this statement. Everyone's family (even nature itself, if you truly consider it) is "dysfunctional", some more than others. While the term "dysfunctional family" is a good colloquialism, it doesn't add up, semantically. If something is dysfunctional, it does not work as 'expected.' (A serious recovering addict never expects to relapse, for example, but very well might, because that's the mechanism put in place by addictions.) These family systems work incredibly well, time and time again, as they were established to; the scapegoat is always blamed, no matter what, an enabler keeps allowing an unhealthy behavior to continue and "the sick person" continues to cause further pain to those who care about them. A "dysfunctional family" is perhaps better termed "a malfunctioning family," because it does not work. It's stuck and keeps glitching in the same fashion, permanently, until it is fixed.

How do we do this, then? What is a family, but a unit of individual human beings? Their family systems come from the small seeds of each individual member, carrying their own pain and issues from their own upbringing as well. Together, each person in the family creates, contributes to and continues the malfunctioning family (that is, the behaviors and the environment). If not all the ingredients are present, this won't happen. Without an enabler, the "sick person" is not tolerated. The family (as a unit and individually) begins to practice self-care.

Until that moment of clarity, that time where we say (and finally mean), "Enough is enough!" We remain trapped by "family traditions" or "generational curses." We as individual pieces of the whole unit have been turned into enablers, or scapegoats; we want to fix the problem and take everything we can, to our detriment, hoping things can be at peace. Soon we become enslaved to other people's affairs, rummaging through their lives till we lose sight of who we are. Suddenly we find ourselves in unfamiliar territory. We are overwhelmed by all we do not know, the things we have not been exposed to or told yet in life. We are unable to survey the ground, see the nets that may entangle us and the traps that lie waiting for us. We have given so much of ourselves to everyone around us, that we come to lose our purpose, lose ourselves. We spend our lives building our identity around others, rather than ourselves, that when the role changes, we become displaced. We then become empty and unfulfilled.

REALITY CHECK: TURN IT AROUND. PUSH IT BACK. TURN AROUND.

When we do, at long last, turn it over, we must be careful what we open our spirit to. Anything that attaches itself to our spirit affects every aspect of our life. Suddenly every move we make is plagued with insecurity and guilt, we find obsessions that were never there, old habits come slowly creeping back into our lives, sour attitudes overtake our positive outlooks or we find ourselves tempted. The enemy likes to hold us in bondage with moods and attitudes. The enemy will make us think that we cannot and will not. Out of desperation, fear and loneliness then we agree, succumb and sleep in the same bed, a sleep of sorrow, in a bed of brokenness. Suddenly when reality comes and wakes us up, we find ourselves in a pool of chaos and calamity. "What's real, was it all a lie? Am I okay now, or in denial still? Can I trust myself again? Can I trust anyone? It's called words of doubt and defeat.

Those words of doubt began to take root after the seed has been planted. Each day, the seed continues to grow (and grow more quickly) with each new day. The warmer the climate and the more the seed is fed, the stronger the root becomes. The stronger the evil spirits overtaking us become and the stronger the sense of confusion when we finally wake up to the truth. Why? Because it draws nourishment from you feeding it or allowing others to flood your spirit with negativity. Toxins and venom begin to build up, preventing us from finding our way and making wise decisions.

While we are allowing others to dump the debris into our lives and letting it all into our spirits, we soon become stuck in the misery. Even if we could move, we have no place to go. Our feet have become weighed down by the mountain of debris that threatens to consume us. Once we have become entangled in the debris, carrying the weight of another's burdens not created by you, but saddled on our back, we soon come to forget our identity. We even lose sight of our purpose, our destiny. The light that once shined so bright in us soon starts to go dim, flickering, threatening to be extinguished permanently. When the light goes out, we lose our way. We can't focus, we are unable to see, leaving us with no clue as to where we are and where we are going... Or how to get there. You need your vision to walk toward your purpose and in to your destiny.

Working in the field of nursing for many years, with people in critical condition, from traumatic injuries to medical illnesses, we carry the torch of caring, nurturing and just want to be part of fixing the problem, with the end result that the sick people we've spent so much time caring for are able to get better, leave the hospital and move on with their lives. But during a crisis, we sometimes see the opposite amongst families. Buried issues soon see the light of day, old pain comes creeping back in, bringing added force to the new pain. Blame and guilt start being exchanged, as secrets start to be whispered again, until they become shouts. Things that they didn't know about their loved ones begin to surface, from hidden medical issues, to illnesses that now require the family as a unit for decision making. Families begin to shift the burden and debris for others to deal with. The pathways, the debris that were missed or forgotten along the way while walking through life have now been found and so we are left trying to figure it out, how to untangle and unravel the broken pieces that were left for us to make sense of.

The more we accept other people's problems in our lives, the more they become comfortable with where they are. While they have a lighter road, this soils the Beauty, the Plan and the Purpose that God has for your life. You lose your place called Peace. Instead of answering our calling and fulfilling our destiny, we're tending to everybody else.

And then the peace we knew and had is lost. We start to absorb the problem of those around us and they begin to manifest themselves in our lives, in the form of anger, irritability, or paranoia. We become so stressed from being over-involved in another's life that is has become "our "life! We cannot, we must not, allow the debris from someone else's life to kill our joy, peace, prayer life, passion, goals, etc., while we are trying to live, trying to reach our potential and fulfill our purpose. We have to refuse to allow their opinions, decisions and experiences to lead us off our path and become tricked into making wrong decisions that will plague us, lose your purpose and die in the process of giving birth to your destiny. Stop looking for affirmations and confirmations. You will find yourself investing your time in things that are not worth your heart. For these are all distractions!

Sometimes, we fall into the entrapment of continuing cycles of abuse, pain and secrets. Without realizing, we use our children to feel good about ourselves. Why? Because we have been used. To us, that system is normal, standard operating procedure. But this does not have to remain "business as usual." We can end it. Our children do not have to become our silent partners. We no longer have to hurt people, because we have been hurt, all in the name of wanting to feel good. It's time to Let It Go and free our spirit from the pain. It's time to turn it around, push it back and let it go.

We must never allow our pain to push us into an identity crisis. What we present is what we become. If we don't like the name we have, we can change it! We are not bound by our mistakes, our losses, or failures, whether they be real or imagined, they are not us and they are not who we are! Never mind our past; never mind where we came from. Never mind that we are shattered from divorce, loss, disease and tragedy. We do not have to remain in brokeness and stuck from the pain of our past and other's problems. Start aligning your name with who are: Victorious, Blessed, Favored, Grateful and Honored. What is your name? The image that you present becomes the narrator of your story. Close the casket, bury those dead issues and breathe life again. No more will we give ourselves excuses, "I don't feel like it," "I started to but," "Something tells me I shouldn't," "I will not be successful." An entire book could be made up of just these excuses! Stop allowing the enemy to use your mind as a battleground. Anger and bitterness spills over into envy, strife, rage, domestic violence, gun violence. Some people when they open their mouth to speak, they spew venom. People who are bitter and distrustful find it easier to compromise who they are and what they believe, with the desecration of their soul with the continued destruction brought about by unresolved trauma. No matter the cost.

Never allow negative and destructive behavior to dominate who you are. No matter where you have come from or what is in your past, you can rise above it.

The turn around begins with a seed. We must get rid of anything that is standing in the way of our growth, our progress and not be hidden away in the darkness, buried by our pain. We must pull back all things that are impure and detrimental to our growth. Anything covered up never grows; likewise, wounds not treated can never heal. So we heal, we show who we are, really are and suddenly we are able to grow again. We have no reason to ever be ashamed of what we have gone through; we have every reason to be proud of what we have overcome.

A healthy tree bears fruit. When there is trauma in the root of the tree, what is supposed to grow and blossom withers and dies from damage. Whatever is connected to the tree dies. The tree is not strong enough to provide the proper nourishment to the branches. When the trauma, when the weeds are removed, when whatever was preventing a life of growth for the tree is exorcised, it first is a shock. The tree has accepted its fate and very quickly, the tree regains its strength.

We cannot continue to look up to our failures, letting our shortcomings set the bar, or be the expectation that we strive for. Losses are not wins! It's time we move on from our failures, moving on to successes, answering the door to the amazing life that is impatiently waiting for us to come outside and start living at last! Stop allowing your failures to become your hero. It is time, truly, to let what has gone by be the furthest thing from our mind. We must focus on the now. Quit looking in the rearview mirror. All we have and need to focus on is what is in front of us now! But we have to be wary. We must not invest our time and heart into something that is going nowhere. It is called a DEAD END!

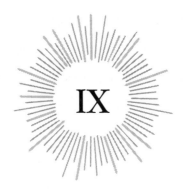

Never Allow The Light That Shines In You To Go Dim

When the light goes out in our lives, we invite darkness to occupy the space it is not suppose to be in. When we allow darkness to occupy our dwelling, our spirit suddenly begins to force-feed negative thoughts, made to walk unbearable journeys, forced to suffer alone in the darkest of places. We no longer operate by faith, but fear, hurt, lack of trust and loathing. Instead of holding our heads high and walking with confidence, we hold our heads down with our face to the floor. We hide behind the curtains of our feelings, refusing to open the window to let reality into our lives. This is the real light, peace, joy and true hope, devoid of the hidden, crooked bargain, we are given through false hope, through addictions and through toxic people. We instead make the same choice, consciously or otherwise, to yet again walk the all-too-familiar broken, trodden path we've circled around our entire lives, not hearing, not listening or acting on what we are being called to do, called towards, called away from circling the drain. We settle, like moments of depression when even showering and putting on clean clothes is too much. We instead opt for convenience and comfort, by draping ourselves in the dirty, rotting, familiar rags of complacency; we tire of attempting in vain to translate the "Divine Plan" and settle on the "Mine Plan."

It is not God who smiles, laughs and rejoices when man plans, but those who would do us harm.

God weeps when man plans, for he knows it ends in our suffering. And as we follow the "Mine Plan," what we think things ought to be like and how we will go about carrying ourselves, impurities slowly creep into our mind, becoming a flood we didn't realize was possible. We assumed the faucet would stop dripping on its own, so there was no need for concern. Distorted thinking becomes the catalyst to unnecessary implosions or explosions, as we find ourselves using hard and harsh words or even physically harming ourselves and others. Yet we continue to fight to discover where we belong in the "Mine Plan." We fight desperately to dust off the ashes that grip our soul and stain our pride, convincing ourselves that this time, we're in control. We become trapped by our emotions, pride and fear being the main blockades, while aching and trying relentlessly to become free, but inevitably failing, for we do not know how to do so; for in the "Mine Plan," we don't even foresee this happening. There is a solution right in front of us, but we fail to see it for admiring our light too much, which ironically is why it goes dim as we begin to falter, stumble and fail. Our pride, our self-focus, our tunnel vision does not even allow us to see when we are in trouble; like a fish, we only see what we longed for, stood on the edge for, cried for, but not the hook it is attached to. This is when the light goes dark, yet again, make no mistake, it is a vicious cycle and has been like this for so long we often don't realize it, even in recovery, until much later in our lives. Allowing your light to flicker and fade allows your spirit to become a servant to negativity. It will turn your sea of blessings into blood, crippling your effectiveness for God. Eventually, bitterness becomes center stage, making you a slave. Your spirit will soon die out, for being starved of love. You begin to feel hindered and unproductive. You feel as if you are fighting in a battle that is getting the best of you. You soon become tired and weary, struggling to get through the day, maybe weeks or months. Such a realization leaves your life open to attacks (spiritual and physical) defeat, weaknesses, pride, distorted thinking and most of all operating outside the Will of God. As your spirit man begins to die out, you soon develop the spirit of a Python.

You may ask what is a spirit of python? A spirit of python is a coiling spirit that once it wraps itself around you, squeezes the life and breath out of you. The python, once they coil themselves around you, their squeeze doesn't shatter your bones, but cuts off your blood supply and suffocates you till you die, emotionally and spiritually. Your blood supply is your lifeline to oxygenate and maintain healthy organs and tissues. A python never chases after its target, instead it catches them off guard. They stay in a camouflage position, waiting patiently. It barrages you with circumstances that knock the wind from you. This spirit will remind you of wounds from your past. It will surround you with ungodly influences and temptations that compromise your character, integrity and the Word of God. It chokes your goals and dreams out of you, leaving you feeling empty. It constricts to keep you from moving forward. They possess a rather unhurried calm attitude in their approach. They lurk in a clandestine manner. It holds you back with attempts to keep you from enlarging your territories to new dreams, goals and business opportunities. It clouds your vision, most of all your spiritual walk. It robs you of your joy and the peace. It chokes your prayer life out of you. You begin to worry about everything and pray about nothing. You start to walk in hopelessness, defeat and fear, instead of faith.

Years ago, I was joined in matrimony with someone that was supposed to be my best friend, soul mate and prayer partner. We would set sail together, with goals on the horizon, that we were excited to reach together. Each milestone would be another plaque on the wall, a celebration and commemoration of all milestones up to and beyond that point, bringing us closer together in love and our faith in God. We would not be afraid to allow the other to shine. After all we were a team, one bulb does not over power another in a light fixture, for they both serve the same purpose and augment each other in doing so.

We were both walking together, on one accord, in the same direction..... Until one day, he drifted off, straying away, off towards another, nearby, different path. Such a realization leaves your life open to attacks, temptation, pride, lovers of themselves more than lovers of God, lust of the flesh, lust of the eye and again operating outside the will of God. You (the mate) are left uncovered and open to attacks of the enemy, when your better half was to keep you covered and protected.

I was desperate to be back on the same course together and I knew that a hard conversation needed to be had between us, none the least of which was this chasm that had been created. As if that wasn't enough, we hadn't discussed for a while the things that married couples needs to discuss, such as retirement, savings, finances, career choices and changes. (And the overarching question, a new home.) The conversation was never took place. There, I was met with complete silence. He had already checked out.

I was no longer the focus or mainstream of his heart. Our relationship no longer held his heart. So each day, the weight was becoming heavier and my light was becoming dimmer and dimmer. I felt life was being choked out of me. I also felt I was developing a "Spirit of Python." I began to feel like I was being suffocated. I was losing the zeal and my vibrancy for life and my goals. I felt as if I was losing sight of what God was calling me to do and mostly my Purpose here on earth. And so, I began to "Fast and Pray." I had to go into that secret Place where I would hear only God's voice and not the voice of man. I knew then I needed God's help. I needed the comfort that only God could bring to me and direction. I needed to grab hold of that anchor that has always kept me secure and connected to my father at any cost. I needed to trust God through this process and know that everything would work out for "My Good and God's Glory." Everything would work out by God's Divine Plan and his Purpose. After all, I belonged to God.

So I sat down and began to take inventory of my life. There I lay all my issues down on the table, seen and unseen, things talked about and the unspoken, everything out before God, asking for help, direction, understanding, clarity, forgiveness and to forgive. Most of all, to let Go of anything that would hinder me from doing what God has called me to do.

It was also then that I realized that I had a hard conversation with myself that needed to be had....

Do I allow this motivation and Determination that is burning inside of me to go out? Should I simply let it die?

Do I allow my goals and dreams to be pushed aside and not birthed out of me to satisfy a stroked ego?

Do I allow my passion and creativity, my work, my lifeblood, to be pushed aside? Am I less important? Is my happiness less important? Are my goals and dreams less important than his?

Do I allow my light to go out? Do I give up, give in and just settle for what is passed on to my plate to make him happy?

Do I pretend to be happy, when I really wasn't happy?

Do you hold on to your mate trying to make him happy when he really is not happy?

There I realized that I would find myself becoming bitter, angry, confused and jealous of the successes of others.

Why?

Because if I allowed my light to go out, this was the light that set sail to "my" dreams and goals. This was the light that held the compass to my destiny. If I allowed this light to go out, who do I trust and who do I put my trust in? How do I raise the level of my faith? How do I leave a legacy for posterity? How do I trust the Word of God when I wasn't willing to reach out and allow God to impregnate me with something so great and be prepared to birth it out?

I needed to fight, I needed to push and push and push until the miracle came forth. I needed to know what I was standing for, take my position and stand, firmly with my feet planted in my rightful place. I needed to not become distracted from what God was calling me to do and what he had called me to be. I needed to take my position and stand tall and strong in God. I needed to be who God had called me to be: "A PROVERBS WOMAN."

A Proverbs Woman is a doer, a helper and a multi-tasker. A Proverbs Woman's first place is in God. She is a leader. She knows her purpose in God. She not only is a busy woman, but a woman who knows that her self- worth comes from her position in God.

When we allow our light to go out, that joy and the peace from the inside is extinguished as well, causing us to settle for things that are not meant to be a part of our life. We find ourselves feeling chronically stuck, trapped in situations trying to figure it all out. The spirit of python then coils itself around you and squeezes the life from you.

With sadness in my eyes and a broken spirit, I soon learned how to dress us my stories. Trying to be happy and smile to the world, when in reality, it was the opposite behind closed doors. I was living in the past of when I was once so happy and the peace that once bared my soul. I was trying to connect back to that happy place that I once shared, but yet remained broken in spirit.

The person that you connect your life with should not be afraid to celebrate with you and be proud of who God has called you to be.

When you have been called for a purpose, it starts with God picking people from your life that are not part of your destiny. We must be mindful and careful who you connect your life to in relationships, friendships and love. You can never change a person's actions, but you can guard your heart. They can restore and bring life or cause you a lifetime of pain and suffering that we are asking God to heal.

Relationships can complement and grow your life or they can slow you down and derail you. When reality sets in, calamity hits. We invest our heart in things that are not worth our heart, better yet going nowhere. It becomes a distraction from our purpose. You then spend years in recovery trying to get your life back. It's not the looks, physique, money that connects you. God uses the Spirit to connect.

As you begin to discover your true purpose, never live beneath your privileges that you begin to live a lie and call it truth.

When God assigns, he designs. As we begin to understand God's purpose and his uniqueness in our lives, we will be able to not allow our light and the things around us to go dull and dim to a point that it goes out. As you begin to understand, walk and live in your Purpose with your Destiny in mind, people will become very uncomfortable with you and around you. God has made you a Designer's Original with He being the manufacturer and not a carbon copy of someone else's life. Blessings will began to overtake you, Healing and Joy overflowing. You can never move away from the Plan of God and count yourself or your life as successful. As you begin to bring in the light, it forces the exit of darkness. Open the gates to allow fear, doubt, unbelief, disbelief, old habits, etc. to exit. "Speak Faith." When you speak faith, you see yourself victorious.

Do not allow yourself to become a victim of unforgiveness. Choose to give up the vengeance in order to walk in Victory. When you forgive, Peace flows and Joy abounds.

When discord, deception, pain, lies arise, put on a garment of praise. Praise was the first tribe in battle. Praise is the recognition that God is still on the throne. Praise lifts you while God is responding to you. The more you praise God and adore him, the brighter your light shines and the stronger he becomes in you.

Stand Strong and hold your light high enough to brighten the dark paths of another person to know that there is hope and life.

Once you choose to let the light in,

CONNECT TO IT

BE IT

WALK IN IT

BREATHE IT

TALK IT

Dorothy Gray

LIVE IN IT

BE CONFIDENT IN IT

IT'S THE NEW YOU...

**"Don't stand in someone else's shadow
when it's your sunlight that should
lead the way."
~ Deanna Blesser**

The Heart of Forgiveness

It takes courage to forgive. We all have things in life that we have had to deal with. Many times when we come from a place of brokenness from childhood, past pain or simply just learning how to navigate through the stages and the different seasons of our life, we haven't quite learned how to separate ourselves from negative people, experiences or emotions. So we act on and react to every negative seed, everything we feel someone has said, done to hurt us or manipulate us. We hold onto these things much too long, even while we are convinced that we have let them go... More often than not, the reason is forgiveness, a Herculean task for certain transgressions. But even more than not, sometimes we just need to hear the words "Please forgive me" or "I'm sorry" and we may well go to the edge of sanity, staring into the dark endless pit before us, just in order to try and hear those words... Even then, they may be empty.

We have gotten to a place where we are using social media to communicate more than ever, but written words simply cannot capture the vagaries of spoken (and better still, face-to-face) communication. Sarcastic becomes snide, desperate turns into destructive and sincerity is shallow, if it even exists. Our patience evaporates, as we've learned to expect an imminent response upon seeing a digital speech bubble form or written indication of thought by way of keyboard. We soak in the words all at once, without the benefit of cadence order, tone and nonverbal cues. We take everything to heart and nothing to heart, as everything changes constantly.... Perhaps we expect human beings to be like technological advances in that regard, but some people do not change.

They poison without purpose, hurt instead of heal and betray instead of befriend. But all of this pain cannot be held on to, not for too long, anyways. Anything we hold inside of us breeds change outside of us. We gain weight, we lose weight, develop twitches, vulgar words becomes our conversations, feelings of being weighted down, anger issues, illicit sexual activity, hatred, low self-esteem, depression, hatred, secret affairs, they walk in fear, they build walls around their heart, afraid to let others in, etc. We even have scars due to self-harm (one step above the final stop on the pain train). All of this pain makes us doubt, scarred and scared we'll again be foolish and susceptible to such attacks. We can't trust others of course, but we soon come to distrust ourselves too. Trust is a luxury we can't afford, so we find ourselves staring at sincerity cynically and analytically, as we search for the true motives behind every word or deed around us. "When does it end?" "Where does it end?" More importantly, how does it end? What if we're unable to hear or accept an apology?

What starts inside, must end inside. We breathe in the hurt. We saturate our spirit with the hurt, we nurture the hurt and we feed the hurt. Our spirit is continuously being fed the root of the hurt till anger, turning to hatred, shows up and takes center stage. It becomes venom. NEWSFLASH: It's a distraction! Push it back! It's a distraction from your purpose! Hatred and unforgiveness allows you to live in a valley of bitterness and unhappiness, which lead to emotional storms. The object of your unforgiveness lives rent free in your head, controlling you. You become locked in a prison without bars. We can't change what has happened to us, but we can either choose to stay in the valley of hatred, unforgiveness, the biblical

Valley of Death or we can choose to rise above it and forgive. Indeed, the Serenity Prayer can be applied here, "Grant me the serenity to accept what I cannot change, the courage to change the things I can and the wisdom to know the difference."

When you can choose to face the spirit of hatred and unforgiveness, you can kill it. When you can face it and choose to forgive, you can heal it. When you choose to eat from the table of hatred, bitterness, resentment, anger, envy, sorrow, jealousy, resentment, despair, pain, rage, revenge and rebellion are your sustenance and you are not able to eat from the seed of love. When you eat from the seed of love, it allows you to grow. Love sees you as you are, then allows you to operate from a position of strength. Whatever you invite into your heart, you have to eat it all. You soon begin to act out or manifest what you have been feeding and nurturing in your spirit. What fruit does unforgiveness bear? Bondage, captivity, poisoned relationships and rage. You soon become captive to the things that you have allowed to control your mind and spirit. It causes you to live in bondage. You soon become a slave to what is capturing and holding your attention. Hatred forces us to re-live old memories; it's not very hard, we have the object living in our head, putting in those old tapes that are most damaging in our hands. We then concentrate on these feelings of hatred, on these memories that can be likened to rusted gold.

There comes a time then, in the process of recovery from the pain, in which we convince ourselves we've rid ourselves (or more accurately, are ridding ourselves) of the memories, as best we are able (though we know this to be impossible, we can fool ourselves for a time) and expurgating the hatred from our souls. We can carry on like this for some time, but one day, something happens to trigger a memory and the tapes play and the hatred flows freer and stronger than ever, as if it was barely contained by a dam that just burst. Strangely, it scares us, but feels good at the same time. This may cause us to be sad and ashamed by the apparent destruction of our progress (though we may also see it as a fake progress, as not. It is simply a reminder we are human; it is silly to expect to banish the hatred from our souls so quickly and in one fell swoop, at any rate, having invited in for so long. After we collect ourselves, we may well realize we are truly done with it now, the hatred and unforgiveness.

So we hide away, yet another box inside of us, out of a sense of obligation, our humanity and yes our hatred (gone or not, and many believe hatred does not vanish, it only hides; the echoes remain) as well. In this box, we hold our judgment towards the object of our unforgiveness. We feel it is natural, excusable, our right and our privilege. Have we truly forgiven, then? We pretend the judgment is based solely out of human concern or compassion, we pretend we have detached, but we clearly haven't. The judgment is taking pleasure, in some degree, of their misfortune. We may create situations where we deliberately hurt them. Both parties have gotten what they want, we now rationalize. An eye for an eye, karma, justice. A lot of times in breakups, divorces, relationships, or the other party has hurt you or has been hurt, When the script of the situation doesn't play out as planned and the other party becomes broken, we rejoice however silently. "Now they know what it feels like" or "They did it to me, so look what happened to them," better yet the all too familiar one "karma is a bi***."

But do we really enjoy this? If we do, (however unlikely it is), that's horrifying. If we don't, which is more often than not, we won't, then what? What has all the waiting and silent wishing for this adversary to fall to their knees done? They won't come back to us (and if they do, it's out of manipulation or feeling powerful and in control, another attempt to settle the score, to rope us back in). We've wasted our time and still had them living in our head this whole time, rent-free! Like generals sending off their soldiers to the battlefield, we've indirectly participated in this, getting even without getting dirty. Whether by purposeful creation of the situation made to harm the other party or solely by thinking about it and staying attached to them still. After all, "an eye for an eye" you reason.

PRETENDING: We pretend that we have forgiven and we are not angry, when we truly are. We have not acknowledged it. So we remain silent. We are not allowed to express how we feel out of fear of being abandoned or left alone. You fear being cast out by someone that you depend on out of a sense of self-worth. You need to stay connected to affirm your self-worth.

"I FORGIVE YOU, BUT I DON'T FORGET WHAT YOU DID." We reheat the sins. In other words, you have lifted the penalty but you will always remember the transgression.

MAKING EXCUSES: You overprotect the person's feelings and become dismissive of our own. You are more terrified of the person leaving you than you are for the sin they commit. So you tolerate. "I understand what has happened to you and why you did what you did." "It was done to you." We make excuses for the person's behavior. Coming to a place of acknowledgement takes courage. Once you acknowledge, you have to own it. Never make excuses for what is wrong, but take a stand for what is right.

UNDERSTANDING FORGIVENESS: Forgiveness can be challenging and at the same time is a changing process. It is bitter but sweet. It requires humility and vulnerability. It involves letting go. It must be honest and operate from a pure place and a made-up mind. Forgiveness forces you to reach beyond where you were and the state of mind that you choose not to stay in. It becomes an attribute that you are becoming stronger. It is something that can never be bought. Forgiveness gives you back your peace and laughter. You began to see things in your life clearly. Forgiveness is a healing balm. It doesn't take the pain away immediately. But it becomes a start of something new.

It gives you the initiative to work toward restoration. Once you have the courage to forgive, you can break the link in the chain that have been holding to your past.

"For if we forgive men, when they sin against you, your heavenly father will also forgive you."
~ Matthew 6:14

In Paul's letters, he cautioned believers against harboring unforgiveness in our hearts toward others. It opens a door and leaves a foothold for the enemy to enter. He wrote:

"In your anger do not sin: Do not let the sun go down while you are still angry and do not give the devil a foothold..." Get rid of all bitterness, rage, anger, brawling and slander, along with every form of malice.

**Be kind and compassionate to one an-
other, forgiving each other, just as in Christ
God forgave you. Be imitators of God, therefore, as dearly loved children and live a life of
love, just as Christ loved us and gave himself
up for us as a fragrant offering and sacrifice
to God.**

~ Ephesians 4:26-27, 31-32; 5:1-2

FORGIVING YOURSELF: Before we can forgive
others and be healed, we must first forgive our self.
We feel the mistake or the pain is too deep to deal
with. The reason why is, we have not figured out
how to heal and forgive ourselves. So we torment
ourselves, which is reflected upon through addictions, self worth, depression, anger issues, over eating.
So we ask the question, "How do I forgive myself?"
The hardest thing becomes the best thing. LETTING
GO. Letting go is the major key to walking free from

the bondage of forgiveness. Bitter but sweet. When you let go of things that cause you not to forgive, you now become stronger each day. Each day you began to peel back layers and layers of what you have been holding on to. We cannot spend our lifetime trying to figure out things that we have no control over. If we continue to flood our present with things of the past, we have no space for the bigger and better things to flow into our lives. So we miss our blessings holding on to the past that hold no benefits to your tomorrow.

We never learn to appreciate, hold on to and cherish what is in front of us. Why? Because we have never let go and chose forgiveness as our recipe to peace and divine restoration. So when a situation triggers the memory of what we have not forgiven or what we are holding on to, we regress emotionally. Whatever the age the initial breakdown happened becomes the age you regress back to emotionally. Many times we take our past pain, failures, mistakes, unforgiveness into relationships with the other party not understanding what we are doing. Forgiveness never became our center point and we have never come to a place of letting go. Many times we attract people into our lives that causes us to re-live a painful past experience through them. The experience becomes a repeat of what has been lying underneath the surface and what we have not forgiven. It becomes a Soul to Soul transaction. Better yet, emotional baggage. The longer you hold on to the space of not forgiving yourself, the larger the web becomes and the baggage becomes that much heavier. You are simply saying, "I have not forgiven myself and the things connected to my past." Release it to God and forgive yourself. When your almighty God has forgiven you, then you must forgive yourself. We must take on courage and affirmations to know, "I will not let people or the pain of my past dominate my future and where I am going".

What seems like your disappointment and disaster turns out to be new direction to something great. Therefore I must let it go.

Once I have forgiven myself, I must now forgive the person or the persons that have hurt me and who I have hurt. I now can smile gain. I have renewed strength. I can now find my purpose in life.

"So, if the Son sets you free, you will
be free indeed."
~ John 8:36

I often think as a child how we used to play tug-of-war with our rope. Both sides began pulling as hard as we could to try and pull the opposite side over to our side. So we began pulling as hard as we can to WIN. We were in war. When someone got tired and let go of the their end of the rope, the war was over.

Release it! "WAR IS OVER!"

WHEN YOU CHOOSE NOT TO FORGIVE: Your choice not to forgive becomes a sign of weakness. It makes you feel powerful and in control, at the same time it becomes a compulsion that cuts you off from life and leaves you soaking in your own hostility and poisonous venom. When you chose not to forgive, it makes you sick spiritually, emotionally and physically. You have then given a voice to your anger and to the other party. "My feelings matter" and "Your feelings are non-negotiable" They have a narcissistic personality. They feel entitled to special rights and priorities. You feel wounded when others do not comply with what you want. When you chose not to forgive, you isolate yourself not just from the person who hurt you, but also people that have done no harm to you. You push every one away.

Unforgiveness restores your pride and ego, but cuts you off from personal growth and a divine walk with God. You never question how you are wrong and the part that you play. When you have chosen not to forgive, you have a fear of facing your own frailties and failures. You soon become an expert on how people have failed you, but never see how you have failed other people.

Forgiveness and unforgiveness never share the same space. The same as darkness and light can't share the same space. When the light begins to shine bright, it drives out darkness. Stop fighting and carrying things that have caused a distraction to what God wants to do in your life. You have failed what the enemy is trying to do in your life. "Sabotage, Confuse, Distract, Rob you of your happiness. Most of all, stop you from finding out "What is my purpose in life?" and detour you from your destiny

One you realize that your past does not dictate your future, and then you forgive and Let it Go. Once our hearts are opened, forgiveness will flow. Forgiveness is a gift to yourself. Forgiveness is not something to simply make you feel better. You forgive in order to feel better and do better.

THE POWER OF FORGIVENESS

IS

"STRONG."

"Jesus said on the cross, "Father forgive them for they know not what they do."

~ Luke 23: 34

Jesus wanted that power to go Forth.

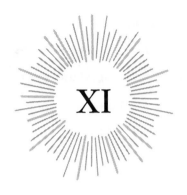

Fabric Of Prayer

"Call Unto Me And I Will Answer Thee And
Show Thee Great And Mighty Things, Which
Thou Knowest Not.
~ Jeremiah 33:3

When we pray, there is a mystery connected to it. Prayer is something that many of us talk about, preach about, read about, but very few of us seem to truly understand prayer or it's Divine connection to the storehouse. Many are unable to grasp the incredible potential of prayer. Prayer has the power to change our circumstances. The Power of Prayer has a way of changing your destiny in life. The tragedy in this is that if we do not understand prayer, we cannot even begin to understand the power of Prayer. Prayer can bring us unattainable peace that we seek, the answers to impossible questions, the solutions to unsolvable problems. It brings clarity and conviction. Prayer is your greatest weapon here on earth. Prayer grants us a serenity that can only come from the Divine. This Divine Peace is a calm unlike anything we can experience otherwise, calling upon Heaven to realize what God wants for us. Power of prayer can transform your life to greater.

I often think about how Fashion Designers rely on textile designers to sit their fashion apart from others. Christian Dior, Versace, Gucci, Givenchy, Burberry, Valentino, Luis Vuitton and Chanel, they are recognized by their signatures. A beautiful piece of fabric, when draped and fitted to couture over our bodies to catch the eye, fit well and becomes instantly recognizable. It stands out over everything and makes a statement from other pieces of fabric. Likewise, the Fabric of Prayer becomes the drape that keeps you covered and protected. It allows you to grow deeper in the Will Of God. It strengthens your confidence. Grants you Grace. Builds intimacy. Affirms his purpose and Emboldens your Faith. It is God's Signature. We are original creations by the ultimate Designer. It complements you and completes you. Many begin to notice an indiscernible difference in the way we carry ourselves and wonder what is so different about you. What has become different is "the Will of God" operating in our lives.

PRACTICE OF PRAYER

It becomes a welcoming table to develop a habit of prayer. PRAYERS DON'T DIE. Through the practice of prayer, we build strength. As we begin to build strength, we continue to exercise our prayer life and develop humility. It becomes a part of our everyday life. Just as food is a necessity for the body, prayer is a necessity to feed your spirit. It is the essential bread of life.

Practice of prayer incorporates a stillness and a silence so that we can hear the voice of God. We grow from an intimacy with God and moving from a conversation with God to Sweet Communion. We learn to rest in his Divine Presence when we spend time with him daily. We no longer see things from our eyes, but through the eyes of God. We take on the heart of God. When we allow the cares of the world to crowd our practice of Prayer, it causes us not to bear fruit.

The practice of prayer becomes our spiritual weapon that enables us to access the throne room. It is then that our prayers transcends boundaries and knows no limits. Prayer becomes a guided missile. An effectual prayer releases a Supernatural Anointing to bombard heaven. You then begin to operate from a position of supernatural strength.

"Let us therefore come boldly unto the throne of grace that we may obtain mercy and find grace to help in the time of need."
~ Hebrews 4:16

"Be careful for nothing; but in everything by prayer and supplication with thanksgiving let your request be made known unto God. And the peace of God, which passeth all understanding, shall keep your hearts and minds through Christ Jesus."
~ Philippians 4:6-7

PROMISE OF PRAYER

It allows us to become peaceful, focused and know that we are in God's will. When we are faced with overwhelming circumstances (doubt, failures, despair, mistakes), we can now see God's love, his strength made perfect in our weaknesses and his faithfulness coming to our rescue in the time of help. There is a comfort that he brings when you are faced with tribulations. This comfort causes your fears, anxieties, worry, doubt, persecution, betrayal, defeat, solitude and despair to dissipate. His Grace steps in to face each problem and address them with supernatural wisdom. You will see your storms clearly and wisely. He backs it up with confirmation. "Yes, this is me speaking to you." Holy Spirit: "I will never leave you or forsake you." The promises of prayer gives us the power to do the will of God, pray with authority and boldness in every situation.

"And if we know that he hears us, whatsoever we ask, we know that we have the petitions that we desired of him."

~ 1 John 5:15

It gives the Believer authority over Satan, your adversary. The enemy will attempt to use weak points and wounds from your past to harass and diminish your effectiveness. He will try and hold you captive to the things of your past. The greatest enemy of your "NOW" world is that you are still holding on to the "OLD" world. You have not been set free from the old DEBT. Stop running and let it GO.

"Humble yourselves therefore under the mighty hand of God, that he may exalt you in due time; Casting all your cares upon him; for he cares for you. Be sober, be vigilant; because your adversary the devil as a roaring lion, walketh about, seeking whom he may devour: Whom resist steadfast in your faith, knowing that the same afflictions are accomplished in your brethren that

are in the world. But the God of all
Grace, who hath called us unto his eter-
nal glory by Christ Jesus, after that ye
have suffered a while make you PER-
FECT, ESTABLISH, STRENGTHEN, SETTLE
YOU to him be glory and dominion
forever and ever."
~ 1 Peter 5: 6- 11

Promise of Prayer opens the door to show you great and mighty things. You will get more accomplished in life in the presence of God and the promise of prayer, than you can in the presence of men.

"Be strong and courageous. Do not be
terrified; do not be discouraged, for
the lord your God will be with you
wherever you go."
~ Joshua 1:9

UNANSWERED PRAYER

Some of us have become frustrated, angry or have turned away from God. We have felt that our prayers or what we have asked God for have not been received. Or it didn't turn out like we wanted it to. Because of this, we now face an obstacle that stands in the way of our faith, trusting God and knowing that all things work together for our good. We have turned away from God and turned to Horoscopes, Psychic Hotlines, Palm readers, cults, metaphysics and tarot readers for our questions to life and in life or to get what we want. Our focus have now turned away from God and turned to materialistic things and worldly ways for instant gratification. "I WANT IT NOW." We shy away from prayer and the things of God to satisfy what we want or how things should work out from our perspective. We jump on the train called unstable. This is a train that moves by the way they are feeling in that moment and they feel as if it is moving in their direction. There are days that the train appears to be moving in a positive direction, so they are happy and full of life. You may hear the words of "God is on my side and I got faith to believe. I NAMED IT, CLAIMED IT and GOT JUST WHAT I WANTED." We to Blessed to be stressed. Everything is good right now. I am living the very life that I wanted. "The Good Life." You may hear many times in a conversation "I am good to people, so good follows me." We have found ourselves attaching to people that we feel are going in the same direction to get what we want or the position that we would like to hold. I called it Social clubs and Social status. But what happens when we wake up in the morning and the train is not moving the way that we see fit in our hearts and mind. The train appears to either have been placed in neutral or it's moving in an opposite direction in our lives. This may happen through tragedy, sickness, disease, loss, barren woman or simply things didn't go as planned they way we thought they should have gone. The manuscript to the good life did not go as planned. "I PRAYED AND PRAYED AND

PRAYED"! We now become confused in our minds about life and the situation. We may even come to a point of almost derailment. We become unstable. We feel as if we are moving backwards at a high rate of speed. The true question lies 'WILL YOU STILL TRUST GOD TO BE YOUR SOURCE"? Are you willing to wait on him? Are you willing to stand alone? So, we start trusting in people, groups, ourselves and most of all other people's opinions to meet our needs and give us worldly advice. We soon start relying on premature conclusions of "why things didn't work out the way we felt they should. We even come to a place that we carry the guilt of "Is it something that I did?" or "What am I doing wrong?" the reason my prayer wasn't answered? So we become isolated and confused. We begun to think in our minds that prayer has not worked in the past, so what is so different about it now? . So they began to delve in ungodly things and activities so satisfy their desires. We become weary. Why? We don't like rejection and most of all we don't like failure. Our relationship with God becomes broken out of frustration leading to bitterness, rebellion, fear, sorrow and despair. We start isolating ourselves from God with the notion that he doesn't care about our problems and most of all "My faith is not strong enough." We become unsure of what we stand for in God and with God. We lose our sense of purpose, we lack direction with a feeling of powerlessness over our situations. Many Christian's prayer lives are suffering today. They become confused about the power and principles of Prayer. They don't understand how to pray and why they must pray. So they start experiencing Poor Spiritual progress, they become weak witnesses for God, we start to take on worldly ways and losing our desire for the things of God and the ways of Our father. We lose that power to transform lives, change circumstances and experience divine peace in the midst of our trials. We lose the power to win souls for the kingdom of God. We start experiencing little Victory over Sin. We soon lose our direction. We become like a ship without a sail, tossing to and fro by every wind that blows our way. Our Ministry becomes unfruitful. Our Love for God becomes least effective in our lives. Our focus becomes the issue that is holding center stage of our lives at that moment. What we lie down to and what we wake up to, is capturing our attention. Be it money, power, success, our personal lives, etc. and what will benefit us. The principles of prayer: Obedience, Truth, Harmony, Humility (He gives Grace to the humble), Gratitude, Thanksgiving (Giving thanks for all things), Faith, the kind of faith that pleases God and ensures answers to our prayers. There are things that God cannot do. "He cannot lie. He cannot worship himself. He will not violate his word and most of all He cannot fail and will not fail."

The good news is, our prayers are meant to be answered or God would have never ask us to pray. It is through prayer that we have gained access to the throne room and the courts of heaven to plead our case before the father. It is our "invitation" from God to his throne room. Prayer does not only involve you communicating with God, but involves God speaking back to you. I often hear many asking the question many times, "I vant to know God's will for my life" and "What am I suppose to be doing here on earth?" The answer lies, "Call upon me and I will answer thee and show thee great and mighty things which thou knowest not."

True prayer is calling forth what has already been pre-destined for our life. True prayer builds your faith till you take God at his word. True prayer operates from a pure place with no ulterior motives or hidden agendas. "Not my will but thy will." True prayer does not try to convince God to do what you want him (God) to do.

True prayer is purpose driven by knowledge of God's will and his ways. We are not driven by impulsion and instant gratification of the "Now." Need it now, Want it now, Got to have it now and do it now so I can move on and move forward. We want quick fixes, quick prayers with quick results.

True prayer must be consistent and persistent. Persistence is connected to learning how to pray and the key to receiving the answers that we need. When we are persistent, we hold tightly to the Word of God. It gives us the Grace, Mercy and the Strength to endure whatever we may face. Satan will hinder us in the earth with attempts to block our prayers through the voice of fear, mind of doubt, heart of disbelief and an unforgiving or heartened heart if we are not persistent. Prayers never die, but they can be hindered.

When you pray, pray with understanding and authority. It is the key to your power. Pray with authority to know that you became as me in your character. You and I became as one.

"That they all may be one; as thou, Father, art in me and I in thee, that they also may be one in us; that the world may believe that thou has

sent me. (22) And the glory which thou givest me I have given them; that they may be one even as we are one."
~ John 17: 21-22

You may ask what does it mean to become as one? You have acknowledged that oneness in God above the world, your problems, your situations, your thinking, your lack, your faith. He wants us to come to him in prayer with gratitude and the attitude of "You are my father and you are the only one that can help me through this." You begin to stand on Truth, which is "God's word" and stand in Truth, which is believing what God has said through faith and standing steadfast being unmovable and unshakeable. Most of all, stand in the Truth of who you are. When you stand in truth, you infuse his Word with truth, which is Prayer. Your words have power, because God has Power. Again,you and I became as one. The more you pray and Praise God, the bigger he becomes in you. The more you begun to lavish and adore him with your words of praise and thanksgiving, the stronger he gets in you. That place of brokeness becomes a place of exposure. The place of brokeness becomes a place to Bless you. The Peace and the Presence of God began to fill you. Your circumstances begin to change. Power, Purpose and your Destiny awaits you. No barriers or closed doors will be able to stop what God has for your life. God's purpose becomes more important than your plans.

"Many are the plans in a man's heart,
but it is the lord's Purpose that prevails."
~ Proverbs 19: 21-22

So the question lies. When you pray whose will are you attending to? "Your will or thy will be done."

"Our Father which art in Heaven

Hallowed be thy name

Thy kingdom come

Thy will be done

In Earth as it is in Heaven."

~ Matthew 6:9-10

When we say "Our Father," we are acknowledging God as our source. You are not speaking about God, you are speaking to him. You are my strength and my redeemer. There is no one above you and no one like you. We have become as one in a sweet communion and intimacy.

When we say "Which art in heaven," we are acknowledging that we need help outside the earthly realm. This is the place that God reigns.

When we say, "Hallowed be thy name," we worship you father as the holy one. We honor you in our lives. Your name is above every name. Hallow means to sanctify. Sacred.

When we say, "Thy Kingdom come thy will be done in earth as it is in Heaven," we are expressing what God wants accomplished for his kingdom. Not my will, but his will on earth. Father rule in my life. Be my king. Establish your kingdom on earth.

"Cause me to obey your will the way the angels obey it in Heaven."
~ Psalms 103:21

Make my obedience a heavenly obedience.

When you open your mouth to speak with authority or are you speaking with words of blasphemy. (Deliberately or inadvertently defame the integrity of someone.)

When you speak the word, are you speaking with expectancy and faith to manifest it? God expects it. It pleasures the heart of God.

WHEN YOU PRAY:

Pray for truth of who you are

Pray for wisdom and understanding

Pray for Clarity

Pray for Unity

Pray for Direction

Pray for Authenticity

Pray for Divine Righteousness

ANSWERED PRAYER

God works in our world to give us peace and teach us patience. Patience to accomplish his purpose and know that God has something greater for us that you can think or imagine. Know that God's timing is not our timing. We discover his will for our life.

Wisdom to know that God has it all in control. He is cultivating persistence and patience while we are building our faith. God wants us to grow in him, know who you are in him. Know that delays are never denials.

God's NO's are never rejection; it's re-direction. His NO's are never punishment. It's preparation for something greater. The more we see Victories in our prayer life, the stronger our faith becomes. God is a prayer-answering God!

When the timing is wrong, God's answer is "SLOW."

When you are wrong, God's answer is "GROW."

"The important things in life are the things that you believe are important "**PRAYER**."

"Prayers outlive the lives of those who uttered them
The lips that uttered them may be closed in death."
~ Arch Bishop Nicholas Duncan Williams

XII

Standing at the crossroads confused and invisible, cloaked in bitterness, broken dreams, buried memories, a past and present that both spell the same pain that consumes our entire soul, heart and mind. Seeing this storm in your mind and trying to discover what you have been called to do in life, but just don't know where to start or where you fit in yet, if at all.

It starts with a renewed mind. It involves you developing a new way of thinking. When you have a renewed mind, the peace of God will always be with you. You will understand the plan and the will of God for your life. You will not only be cleaned up on the outside, but transformed on the inside. He will guide you into all truth. A renewed mind calls us to reach higher standards, filtering our thoughts and emotions and placing boundaries. "Right thinking leads to Right feelings and Right Feelings leads to Right Actions."

"And be not conformed to this world: but be ye transformed by the renewing of the mind, that ye may prove what {is} that good and acceptable and perfect, will of God."
~ Romans 12:2

When you have a renewed mind, No weapon that is formed against you can stop you and no devil in Hell can hold you.

When you can uncover and face your past, you can understand your present. Before I could move forward, I had to understand my past. Before I could understand everything that was happening around me and in my life, I needed to understand my past. Not to regret, hate, focus on deep-seated pain, but to understand my past. The hardest place to trust God is in that broken place. But in that broken place is where you will meet God. God did not allow you to go through the pain to curse you and leave you, he allowed you to go through to establish a closer relationship with you. Standing in that broken place does not mean that you have to remain in brokenness and in that broken place. As we become secure in our relationship with the father, we begin to allow our past to fall from us like a garment. "It doesn't fit." We then chose not to wear it. God wants to heal you, bless you, lift you up and strengthen you. Where there is a relationship will be fruit. We learn to rest in the promises of God. As you learn to rest in the promises of God, it is your faith that becomes stronger. You look to the invisible, indescribable, omnipresent God to do the impossible and be confident in the new you. No matter where you are in your journey, God has enough Grace to meet you there and carry you through your suffering with endurance. His Grace will sustain you. Grace will meet you in your pain and allow you to over-come any circumstances. Grace lifts you above your disappointment and pain.

Love embraces you, covers you, fills you up, so he can create a new life of peace and happiness for you. It becomes a motivator. Loves meets you where you are in your circumstances and sees you as you are. Love breaks through the barricades.

God will give you strength to build on things that will last and never give up or give in just to sur-vive. Strength to keep moving forward, onward and upward, press on and to push past your issues and to climb mountain after mountain. Strength to overcome all of the pain and through all of it... Shine, hold on to your faith, for without faith, we let go, succumb and lose to it. We fail. We die. Hope, love and faith however, can keep us running, even if merely on fumes, until we find a reason to live. A passion, a purpose, sometimes even a person for a time can be that, but be wary of assigning someone that power over you long-term, as noted.

When you discover your passion, your purpose becomes very clear and suddenly your unique destiny is a bit easier to see... You are starting to find your way, learning to love yourself. Happiness becomes your fragrance that you arise to. You are learning to embrace change and making each day your best day. You cannot change your yesterday, but you must accept the lessons learned. Allow the mistakes of your past to remain in the shadows of time gone by. Your life involves everything that encircles you. We must learn to stop judging and learn to understand, not to restrict our emotions, but express them. Take the limit off God. No matter what challenges we face, God will give us the peace to know that "he is always in control." Don't lose your focus. You smile at the sun on your face and feel joy in the birds chirping.

You're awake. It's a new day and you're going to be just fine. Doubt will become strong faith, discouragement will become empowerment and your peace and your despair will become your Purpose and Fulfillment. Allow Goodness and Grace to flow through you with God revealing his Master Plan for your life.

A new day awaits you.

CELEBRATE: IT'S THE NEW YOU!

Photography by Arjay Moreno

About the Author

When author **Dorothy Gray** isn't busy saving lives as a Registered Nurse, she's busy writing. Dorothy divides her time between California and Florida, both of which she calls home. She is grateful to God for her writing ability, her nursing skills, and her passion for these two aspects of her life. Dorothy also finds time to be a life coach, which she accomplishes as founder and CEO of Destined and Determined. It's just one more way in which she can help people, as helping people, whether through writing, nursing, or life-coaching, is her mission.

Dorothy says, "My greatest blessing is a cultivating heart in which humility, patience, faith, and wisdom can take root and flourish, which produces a shelter for others." Dorothy's inner strength and Divine peace are characteristics of confidence—not in herself, but in God, and the ability to hear his voice. Dorothy is definitely all about empowering and inspiring people. Healing is her ministry.

40387501R00134

Made in the USA
San Bernardino, CA
18 October 2016